The Digital Guide to Software Development

Corporate User Publications Group / Digital Equipment Corporation

 ™

Digital Press

9 8 7 6 5 4 3

Printed in the United States of America.

Order number EY-C178E-DP
ISBN 1-55558-035-1

Editors: Michael Catano, Dean Fachon, H. Jim Hager
Manuscript Editor: Kathe Rhoades
Illustrator: Lynne Kenison
Compositor: Corporate User Publications (CUP/ASG),
           Digital Equipment Corporation

The following are some of the trademarks and registered trademarks of Digital Equipment Corporation; third-party trademarks and other Digital Equipment Corporation trademarks are listed in the back of the book.

DEC	MASSBUS	RT
DECmate	PDP	UNIBUS
DECUS	P/OS	ULTRIX
DECwriter	Professional	VAX
DIBOL	Rainbow	VMS
digital™	RSTS	VT
	RSX	Work Processor

This book was prepared using VAX DOCUMENT, Version 1.1.

Contents

TABLES

Preface

There are many approaches to developing software products. This book provides insight on how engineering teams develop software at Digital Equipment Corporation.

The suggestions offered here are based on our accumulated experience in turning software concepts into successful products. Through the development of the VMS operating system and its many layered products, Digital's development community has learned a great deal about using structured software development and programming standards to deliver high-quality products.

The Digital approach to software development is called the phase review process. This process divides the life cycle of software products into six phases and provides a set of measurable events for each. In this way, the software development process is divided into more manageable pieces.

The Digital Guide to Software Development was written for individuals seeking information about a practical, efficient, and standardized approach to the software development process. These individuals include software development managers and engineers, software technical writers, and those studying software engineering. This book concentrates on the activities of the software development team and the phases in which they are most interested and most involved.

The software development cycle used at your company may be quite similar to or somewhat different from the process described here. However, if you are looking for ways to enhance productivity throughout your development process, this book can help you in two ways:

1. Over the life cycle of a software product, it is easier and cheaper to develop and maintain the software if you use a structured and practical software development methodology, such as the phase review process.

2. The productivity of your software development team can be increased if you use a wide spectrum of software development tools to implement your methodology. This book discusses the tools used at Digital that are also available to you.

This book is organized as follows:

- Chapter 1, The Digital Phase Review Process, introduces the phase review process used at Digital for developing software applications and provides a brief description of each phase.

- Chapter 2, Software Development Tools, reviews the software development tools used at Digital. You can use these tools in your software development efforts.

- Chapter 3, Project Management, provides guidelines for managing a software development project. This chapter emphasizes the team approach to software development. It also discusses the role and responsibilities of project team members from a variety of functional groups such as software engineering, marketing, manufacturing, and customer services.

- Chapter 4, Planning and Preliminary Design, details the tasks you perform in the preliminary stages of software development to get your project off to the right start. Tasks discussed include high-level design, design methodologies, design reviews, and standards.

- Chapter 5, Design and Implementation, is the first of three chapters devoted to the design and implementation phase. This chapter discusses developing base levels and build procedures for base levels.

- Chapter 6, Coding Guidelines for Implementation, focuses on coding guidelines for implementing the detailed software design. This chapter includes information on selecting coding guidelines, methods of improving code readability, choosing an implementation language, conducting code reviews, and naming conventions.

- Chapter 7, The Testing Process, concentrates on the testing processes used to verify an implementation against its design. It discusses the levels of testing you need to perform, the types of tests to perform, and some approaches to designing tests.

- Chapter 8, Qualification, presents procedures for field testing the product and qualifying it for final production.

- Chapter 9, Maintenance, provides some guidelines for minimizing maintenance costs associated with developing a software product. Maintenance costs can account for a significant portion of engineering resources throughout each phase of software development.

- Appendix A, Coding Conventions for VAX C, provides guidelines for coding software using the C programming language. By using the guidelines discussed in this chapter, you can take the steps needed to increase the portability of your software product and decrease the costs of your development efforts.

- Appendix B, International Product Development, presents a model for creating a product for an international market. This is becoming more important in today's global marketplace.

- Appendix C, Industry Standards, summarizes IEEE standards and other nonproprietary standards.

- Appendix D, Additional Reading, contains the name and order number of a variety of Digital documents discussed in this book. It also contains information about other helpful books.

Chapter 1

The Digital Phase Review Process

Developing software applications is a labor-intensive activity. The size and complexity of software applications continue to increase, and user expectations of software applications have grown more sophisticated. For these reasons, the difficulty of managing software development activities has continued to increase, as have the personnel costs of software development and maintenance.

To effectively deal with these issues, Digital has developed an approach to software development called the phase review process, illustrated in Figure 1–1. This process has the following basic characteristics:

- It divides the life cycle of a software product into six phases.

- It identifies a set of plans, activities, and documents that are reviewed at the end of each phase before moving on to the next.

- It brings together participants from key functional groups at the end of each phase to determine whether the project has met its goals for the phase and whether the project should proceed as planned.

This chapter introduces the phase review process, describing in general terms the activities and responsibilities associated with each phase. Succeeding chapters provide more information on phases highlighted in Figure 1–1. These are the phases in which the software development team are most involved.

Figure 1–1:   The Phase Review Process for Product Development

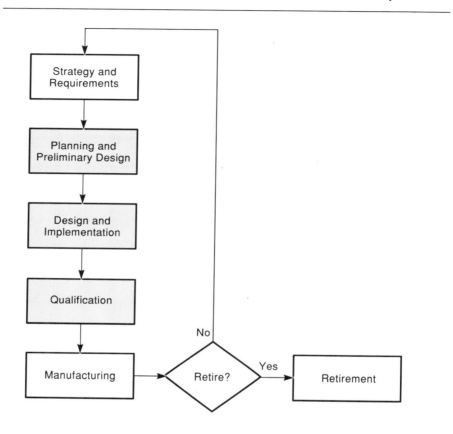

The phase review process defines the project life cycle over six phases. The life cycle begins with the identification of a product opportunity that is consistent with the company's product strategy. The product requirements are clearly defined, the preliminary design is established, and then refined and implemented. The product is qualified by field testing and, when ready for release, sent to manufacturing for duplication. The life cycle ends with an integrated plan to retire the product.

Ideas for software products come from a variety of sources. Sometimes the impetus comes from engineering; other times it comes from marketing. Sometimes the product is more than an idea; it may already be in use on a small scale in an internal group. Sometimes it may be an adaptation of an existing software product. In any case, when a product is to become a company product, a product team is formed. Then, the product and the product team are submitted to the discipline of the phase review process.

The product team is led by a product manager who guides the project through all of its development phases. At Digital, the typical product team includes representatives from the following functional groups:

- Engineering
- Product management
- Finance
- Manufacturing
- Customer services
- Marketing
- Sales

The phase review process provides an operational guideline for managing a product through its life cycle. The process provides a common set of planning, measurement, and implementation tools to help product teams deliver high-quality systems to customers. Each phase has a set of required plans, activities, and documents. The process is simple, dynamic, and flexible. It encourages and facilitates effective cooperation and commitment among the cross-functional groups. The process helps ensure that the necessary documents exist and are reviewed by the appropriate people and groups. It also improves the discipline and predictability required to effectively develop and deliver the final product.

A key feature of the phase review process is the formal review held at the end of each phase. At this time, the product manager convenes a phase review meeting to determine whether the product has met the milestones for the current phase and is ready to move to the next one. Attendees include managers and key contributors from each functional group represented on the product team. This meeting is a critical one. At this forum the software engineers and other functional groups review the status of the project, demonstrate that the product performs according to its plans, and agree on any changes that may be needed before moving on to the next phase.

This book concentrates on phases for which the software engineering development team is principally responsible. These include the following, each of which is highlighted in Figure 1–1 and described in greater detail in succeeding chapters:

- Planning and Preliminary Design
- Design and Implementation
- Qualification

In the remaining sections in this chapter, however, we will briefly discuss every phase in the Digital phase review process in order to provide the context.

1.1 Strategy and Requirements Phase

The strategy and requirements phase marks the start of a product's development life cycle. The primary activity during this phase is to investigate a specific market need that has been identified. The product team assesses the feasibility of technical options, market risks and strategies, and product requirements.

In planning strategy and requirements, the product team considers technical approaches to building the intended product. Individuals outside the immediate product team are consulted for their expertise in relevant areas. Often, possible solutions to difficult technical problems are prototyped to make sure the implementation risks are well understood. By the end of this phase of development, the system is generally defined, and a business decision is made on whether to proceed.

During the strategy and requirements phase, the members of the product team share the following responsibilities:

- Funding the project
- Proposing a product that is consistent with the company's strategy
- Building a coordinated plan that incorporates subordinate plans from all functional groups
- Planning for the manufacturing and production process

- Providing marketing information
- Developing service requirements and sales strategy

Product team members also have specific individual tasks, which are described in more detail below. Figure 1–2 summarizes the tasks and documents that are a part of this phase.

- *Product manager*

  With input from all members of the product team, the product manager prepares a preliminary business plan outlining the product's priorities, goals, market needs, international requirements (if any), and projected financial costs and sales. Similarly, the product manager also prepares a product requirements document that outlines the technical requirements of the product.

- *Marketing project manager*

  Prepares a marketing requirements statement that demonstrates an understanding of the market in which the proposed product will compete.

- *Engineering project leader*

  Leads the engineering development team (described in Chapter 3). The engineering development team reviews the technical feasibility of the product and prepares a list of alternatives. Typically, the team begins work on several documents necessary for planning and preliminary design:
  — Preliminary product specification
  — Preliminary development plan
  — Preliminary documentation plan

- *Customer services representative*

  Prepares the customer services impact/requirements statement, which analyzes how the product requirements will affect the customer services group.

- *Sales representative*

  Prepares the sales impact/requirements statement, which outlines the product sales support requirements and tools needed to support the product.

Figure 1–2: Strategy and Requirements Phase

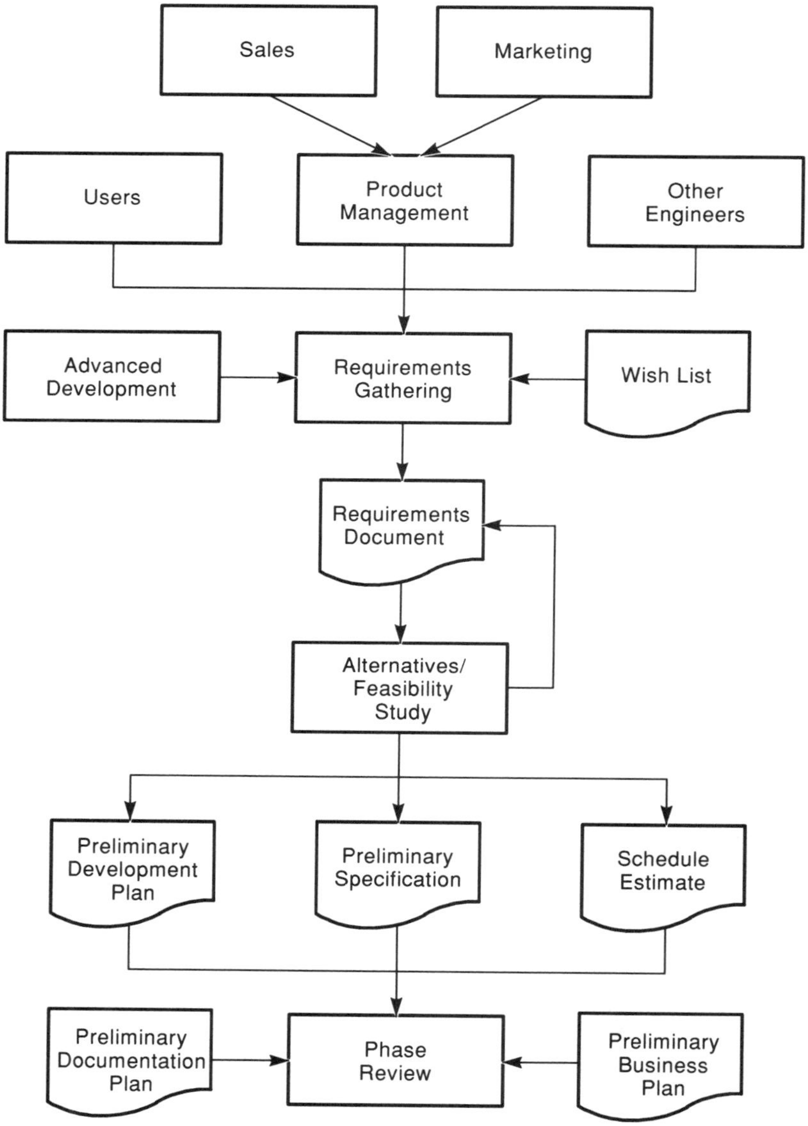

- *Manufacturing project manager*

  Prepares the manufacturing impact statement, if necessary, which analyzes how the product will affect the manufacturing group.

- *Finance representative*

  Prepares a financial needs statement and maintains administrative control over budgeting.

See Chapter 3, Project Management, for additional information on the members of a product team and project documentation.

1.2 Planning and Preliminary Design Phase

The objectives of planning and preliminary design are to create complete product specifications, a preliminary design, and an integrated project-implementation plan. This plan helps ensure that the commitments made by all functions involved in the project can be achieved.

During this phase, the product manager updates the business plan to reflect the input from the entire development team. The engineering project leader distributes the engineering plan, which contains the product specification, the development plan, and a schedule. The engineering plan defines how and when the product will be built, tested, and delivered.

The software engineering development team also prepares a verification test plan. This plan describes how the product will be tested and verified to comply with the product specification, the manufacturing plan, and the support guidelines.

Representatives from marketing, sales, customer services, and technical documentation prepare documents outlining plans and strategies for meeting the product's requirements within their respective groups. These plans contain sections on how to sell and support the product, deliver training, and develop and deliver user documentation.

Chapter 4, Planning and Preliminary Design, contains more information on planning and preliminary design.

1.3 Detailed Design and Implementation Phase

The objective of the detailed design and implementation phase is to execute the plans made during planning and preliminary design. The product design is completed and the product is coded and verified by internal testing. The goal is to demonstrate that the product has met the product specifications and design.

During this phase, members of the product team update their respective plans to reflect any changes. Team members also submit their respective product support plans. Plans for field testing are finalized.

More information about the design and implementation phase is included in the following chapters:

- Chapter 5, Design and Implementation
- Chapter 6, Coding Guidelines for Implementation
- Chapter 7, The Testing Process

1.4 Qualification Phase

The objective of qualification is to field test the product at selected external sites representing a cross-section of customers. The field test process should demonstrate, through testing and feedback, that the product meets its requirements and specifications. By the end of this phase, the development team has master copies of the final product ready to send to the manufacturing group for duplication and distribution to customers.

During this phase, product team members update their plans, and the development team ensures that the product is ready for release:

- The product manager, along with the development manager, ensure that the product performs to specification and is ready for manufacturing and shipping to customers.
- The documentation manager verifies that the product documentation is complete and technically accurate.
- The manufacturing manager confirms that the product meets the minimum criteria for shipping the product to customers.

Chapter 8, Qualification, has more information on qualifying the design for production.

1.5 Manufacturing Phase

When a product is ready for manufacturing, the master copies of the software and documentation are given to the production group for duplication. The product is then mass produced, packaged, delivered, and serviced in a way that is satisfactory to customers.

Market performance evaluations are conducted periodically to determine if the planned market and product goals are being achieved. The results of this evaluation are used as part of the decision to continue, enhance, or retire the product from the marketplace.

1.6 Retirement Phase

A product enters the last phase of the life cycle when it is to be retired. The objective of the retirement phase is to phase out all marketing and manufacturing responsibilities and transfer all service-related manufacturing responsibilities to the customer services organization. A product is phased out in a manner that fulfills any internal and external commitments.

At retirement, the phase-out plan is reviewed, the customer base is migrated to replacement products, and the product is phased out. The various groups stop supporting the product. The product team plans how the phase-out will be handled, what will be done with any existing product inventory, and what strategy will be used to phase out services of the product.

Chapter 2

Software Development Tools

The demand for more complex, high-quality software is growing at an unprecedented rate. As software becomes a more important part of the products and services that businesses offer, and plays a more important role in the management of business, the ability to match the demand for software development and maintenance is now crucial. In an attempt to meet these demands, Computer Aided Software Engineering (CASE) has emerged.

This chapter provides an overview of a number of CASE tools and other software tools used at Digital to implement various elements of its software development process. At Digital, CASE is an integrated set of software tools and services that enable efficient implementation of disciplined software engineering methodologies and procedures. The Digital CASE environment contains a set of integrated tools for designing, coding, testing, and maintenance of complex software applications, as well as for project management, documentation, and communication among developers.

Although tools cannot solve all the problems of software development organizations, they help developers accomplish the following goals:

- Create a more predictable and disciplined development process
- Create high-quality, error-free software
- Achieve greater efficiency in the development process
- Reduce time-consuming maintenance tasks
- Complete a software project as specified
- Deliver a finished software product earlier

The integrated software development tools available for the VMS operating system provide an especially rich and robust environment for software development. Figure 2–1 associates some of the tools discussed in this chapter with the stages of the project development in which they are used.

2.1 Software Development Tools

Problems most often faced by programmers today fall into three basic categories. Programmers must increase their programming output, improve its quality, and manage the complexity of their programming tasks. The tools discussed in this section can help meet each of these challenges. At Digital, programmers use the following tools to help them design, code, build, test, and maintain software:

VAXset
VAX Language-Sensitive Editor
VAX Source Code Analyzer
VAX DEC/Test Manager
VAX Performance and Coverage Analyzer
VAX DEC/Code Management System
VAX DEC/Module Management System
VAX SCAN
VAX CDD/PLUS
VMS Debugger

2.1.1 VAXset

The VAXset software is a package of six integrated tools designed specifically to automate many of the repetitive tasks of software development. These tools, discussed in the next sections, include:

VAX Language-Sensitive Editor
VAX Source Code Analyzer
VAX Performance and Coverage Analyzer
VAX DEC/Test Manager
VAX DEC/Code Management System
VAX DEC/Module Management System

Figure 2–1:   VMS Tools for Software Development

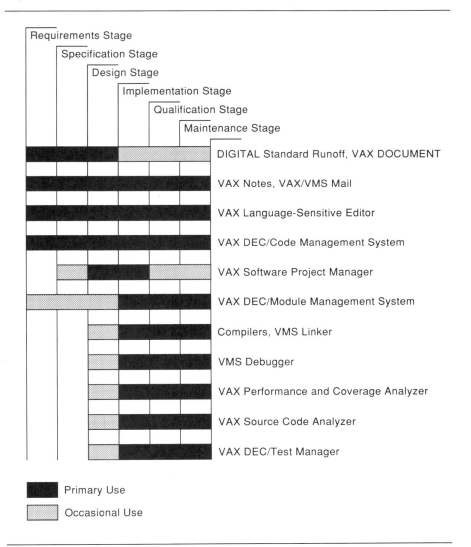

For information on using the VAXset tools together to develop software applications, see *A Methodology for Software Development Using VMS Tools.*

2.1.2 VAX Language-Sensitive Editor

In today's environment, software engineers need a productivity tool that can help them code faster and more accurately, regardless of their experience level. Digital's software engineers use the VAX Language-Sensitive Editor software (LSE) to develop and maintain source code. LSE is a multilanguage text editor that provides source code templates for each language it supports. These templates help both the novice and the experienced programmer build programs faster, using the correct syntax and punctuation.

With the editor's language templates, engineers can create an entire skeletal structure by successively expanding keywords (called tokens) and placeholders. Placeholders specify positions within the template at which an engineer must either choose an option from a menu or enter program code. For example, suppose a user wants to enter a WHILE loop in a Pascal program. To do so, the user types the WHILE keyword and then expands that construct by pressing the "expand" key. In response, LSE produces the following text:

```
WHILE %{expression}% DO
    %{statement}%
```

Within this template, there are two placeholders: one for the Boolean expression, *%{expression}%*, and one for the statement that forms the loop body, *%{statement}%*. In this example, pressing the expand key when the cursor is on *%{statement}%* displays a list of valid Pascal statements. The user can then choose the desired statement or type over the placeholder to replace it with the desired program code.

LSE provides the following features:

- Provides source code templates for the constructs in the following VAX programming languages and products:

    VAX Ada
    VAX BASIC
    VAX Bliss–32
    VAX C
    VAX CDD
    VAX COBOL
    VAX DATATRIEVE
    VAX DIBOL
    VAX DOCUMENT

VAX FORTRAN
VAX MACRO
VAX Pascal
VAX PL/I
VAX SCAN
VAXELN Pascal

- Tailors the editing sessions for each of the VAX languages and products that support LSE
- Uses source code templates that are both formatted and language-specific to enter source code quickly and efficiently
- Allows coding, compiling, reviewing, and correcting of compile-time errors without leaving the editing session
- Provides interactive editing capabilities during a debugging session
- Allows engineers to tailor the defined language environments or to define their own environment
- Provides integrated access to the cross-referencing features of the VAX Source Code Analyzer (see Section 2.1.3)

In short, LSE enables programmers to produce syntactically correct code even if they do not know the language very well.

For more information on LSE, see the *Guide to VAX Language-Sensitive Editor and VAX Source Code Analyzer*.

2.1.3 VAX Source Code Analyzer

The VAX Source Code Analyzer software (VAX SCA) helps Digital software engineers understand the complexities of a large software project by allowing them to make inquiries about the symbols in its source code. This tool works with supporting compilers to provide multilanguage, interactive cross-referencing and static analysis. With VAX SCA, engineers can move easily through all the project's files, quickly locating the definition of any symbol name or any references made to that symbol name.

Using the cross-referencing capabilities of VAX SCA, engineers can display information about program symbol names in their source files. The FIND command greatly simplifies the following cross-referencing tasks:

- Locating symbol names and the occurrences (other uses) of the names
- Locating a specified set of names or partial names; wildcards are permitted
- Locating symbol names based on their specific characteristics (such as routine names, variable names, or source files)
- Locating symbol names based on their specific occurrences (such as the primary declaration of a symbol, read or write occurrences of a symbol, or occurrences of a file)

For example, the cross-referencing capability of VAX SCA allows engineers to quickly find all the locations where a symbol name is used throughout an application, thus helping them to better understand the results of any changes to a symbol name. VAX SCA eliminates the need for searching through hard-copy listings for symbol names.

Engineers can get information about program structure, that is, the interrelation of routines, symbols, and files by using the static analysis capabilities of VAX SCA. Static analysis features include the following:

- Routine call relationships are displayed relative to a specified routine.
- Routine calls are analyzed for consistency, with specific regard to the numbers and data types of arguments passed and the types of values returned.

For more information on VAX SCA, see the *Guide to VAX Language-Sensitive Editor and VAX Source Code Analyzer*.

2.1.4   VAX DEC/Test Manager

During the design and implementation phase, development teams must ensure that the application being developed performs to specification. The VAX DEC/Test Manager software organizes software tests and automates the way tests are run and results are evaluated. To use DEC/Test Manager, software developers first write test scripts for their software: each test script consists of input to the software that will test various software functions. As the software is run under each test script, the DEC/Test Manager captures the output.

DEC/Test Manager is based on the concept of regression testing. Regression testing is a method of ensuring that software in development runs correctly and that newly added features do not affect the correct execution of those previously tested.

In regression testing, the development team runs established software tests to compare the current test results with previously established benchmark results. These benchmark results must be duplicated if the software is functioning properly. If the current results do not match the benchmark results, the current software may contain errors. The software is said to have "regressed" in that it does not conform with previously established behavior. In this case, the current software version needs to be reworked.

DEC/Test Manager has the following features:

- Lets engineers create scripts of software tests
- Sets up the test environment so that tests are executed under controlled conditions
- Executes specific tests, groups of tests, and combinations of test groups, either interactively or in batch mode
- Compares the results of each executed test with its benchmark test results to determine differences
- Records an interactive terminal session and associates it with a test description
- Allows engineers to group test descriptions into meaningful combinations for later runs
- Allows engineers to examine test result files interactively
- Generates summary reports of test set runs

For more information on DEC/Test Manager, see the *Guide to VAX DEC/Test Manager*.

2.1.5   VAX Performance and Coverage Analyzer

The VAX Performance and Coverage Analyzer software (VAX PCA) is another tool that is used during testing. Engineers use VAX PCA to analyze the run-time behavior of an application under development. It analyzes test coverage by measuring which parts of an application are or are not executed by a given set of test data. Engineers use this information to create tests that thoroughly exercise the application. VAX PCA also pinpoints execution bottlenecks and other performance problems. Using this information, the development team can modify modules to run faster.

VAX PCA can collect, analyze, and report on the following types of data:

- Program counter sampling data—Provides a good overview of where a program consumes the most time.
- Page fault data—Helps determine what sections of the program cause the most page faults.
- Exact execution counts—Provides the exact number of times a program executes specified locations, thereby helping the team to understand a program's dynamic behavior.
- Test coverage data—Shows which code paths are or are not executed during testing.
- System services data—Shows which sections of the program call system services.
- Input/Output data—Details all VMS Record Management Services (VMS RMS) calls in a program, thus helping development teams to understand a program's input/output behavior. VMS RMS software is a data management tool that provides an interface at the application-program level to record and file management functions.

For more information on VAX PCA, see the *Guide to VAX Performance and Coverage Analyzer*.

2.1.6 VAX DEC/Code Management System

Maintaining software configuration management and keeping track of source code files during development are tough challenges for any software development team. If the wrong version is linked or the latest changes are lost, the team can lose days or even weeks trying to correct the problem. To overcome such problems, development teams at Digital use the VAX DEC/Code Management System (DEC/CMS) software to coordinate source code files. DEC/CMS software is used to ensure that the files are always up-to-date and available, and to construct software versions.

The DEC/CMS software is a tool that all team members can use—managers, system analysts, technical writers, and engineers. At Digital, engineers use it to organize and maintain all their program source files. They also use it to track everything that happens to project files during development. DEC/CMS records every change, the reason for the change, who made it, and when.

DEC/CMS can also be used to merge modifications and store current and historic versions of the files in a central library. Using the class feature of DEC/CMS, development teams can associate a unique DEC/CMS class name to each file and element related to a specific software version. Thus, the class identifies all the files and elements related to a specific version and provides a method of proper software configuration management.

DEC/CMS can store any binary file, including a project's object files and its executable images. The code management aspects of software configuration management are especially important on large projects that develop over a long period of time and have multiple versions of the developing software.

DEC/CMS works on any file created with an editor. Team members use it to store documents, plans, specifications, status reports, or other records.

In summary, DEC/CMS performs the following functions:

- Keeps track of files at every phase of development
- Monitors changes in files to avoid conflict
- Allows team members to concurrently work on the same file without the risk of losing the changes made by any team member, while reporting any conflicts
- Conserves disk space as it stores the source files for documentation and code
- Supplies source material for generating project activity reports
- Maintains a history of library activity
- Stores files from other software development tools

For more information on DEC/CMS, see the *Guide to VAX DEC / Code Management System*.

2.1.7 VAX DEC/Module Management System

When building a software system, engineers must include the correct version of each software component. To maintain proper software configuration management at Digital, software engineers use VAX DEC/Module Management System (DEC/MMS) software. DEC/MMS provides a consistent means of automating the building of modular software applications, from simple programs of one or two files to complex programs consisting of many source files, message files, and documentation. DEC/MMS software builds a system faster because it builds only the parts that require building. No time is wasted in recompiling and linking modules that have not changed since the previous system build.

After DEC/MMS is set up to handle a software application, it can build the application with one command. DEC/MMS then manages the system build by retrieving the proper version of each source code file from a DEC/CMS library.

DEC/MMS provides the following features:

- Builds only the parts that need building, thereby building the system more quickly
- Consistently reproduces the same system each time it is built, thereby increasing the accuracy of the build

For more information on DEC/MMS, see the *Guide to VAX DEC/Module Management System*.

2.1.8 VAX SCAN

Development teams frequently need to reformat or transform existing source files and other project files to match the standard used on the current project. Also, a team might need to translate the program source code from one language variant to another, for example from DECSYSTEM–20 BASIC–PLUS–2 to VAX BASIC. The VAX SCAN software helps programmers create tools to solve such cumbersome and time-consuming text-processing tasks.

The VAX SCAN programming language is designed to help software development teams create their own text-processing tools, that is, tools that manipulate text strings and files.

The features of VAX SCAN include the following:

- Implemented as a high-level language
- Has extensive string-processing capabilities, including operators for complex pattern matching
- Capable of calling VAX SCAN routines from other VAX languages
- Capable of calling routines written in other VAX languages from VAX SCAN
- Capable of calling the VMS Run-Time Library (RTL) and System Service routines from VAX SCAN
- Integrated for use with the VMS Debugger
- Integrated for use with LSE

The program created with VAX SCAN contains statements that define the following:

- Rules for building "tokens" from the characters in the input stream
- Rules for defining patterns of tokens that are to be recognized in the input stream
- Actions performed by the application when it recognizes a pattern

The input and output streams of text can be defined as a file, a string, or a routine address, which can be called back to obtain the text. Thus, VAX SCAN applications can be designed either as independent applications or as part of larger systems.

VAX SCAN rules for building tokens and for defining and recognizing grammars (patterns) help developers create applications more quickly than is possible with a traditional programming language such as COBOL or Pascal. Thus, VAX SCAN gives developers the potential to create applications to solve problems that were left unresolved in the past.

Another feature of VAX SCAN is that it is a compiled rather than an interpreted implementation. Because it is compiled and conforms to the VAX Procedure Calling and Condition Handling Standard, VAX SCAN procedures can easily be integrated with procedures written in other languages and system services. (This standard describes the techniques used by all VAX languages for invoking routines and passing data between them. See Section 4.6.1 for more information.)

For more information on VAX SCAN, see the *Guide to VAX SCAN*.

2.1.9 VAX CDD/PLUS

Managing data requires significant time and effort in application development, especially when two or more applications need to share some common data. The need for a central repository of data definitions has gained increased recognition in recent years. Incorrectly defined data is a major source of errors and delay in the development process; applications programmers need accurate definitions.

At Digital, software development teams use the VAX CDD/PLUS (Common Data Dictionary) data base. VAX CDD/PLUS permits data administrators to store accurate and complete definitions in a central location accessible to all. VAX CDD/PLUS efficiently helps manage and control definitions across the modules that make up an application. By planning for its use early in a project, a team can simplify its management tasks.

VAX CDD/PLUS software is designed to be used throughout the life cycle of a software development effort. It stores data definitions common to many separate programs, which may be written in many different languages. CDD/PLUS is particularly well suited to commercial environments where multiple application programs access large central data bases.

By storing data definitions in a central repository, VAX CDD/PLUS provides the following benefits to a project:

- Eliminates the need to define data within application modules.
- Reduces redundancy (multiple copies of the same data definitions) and inconsistency. To change a data definition that affects several application modules, the user needs to make the change only once in VAX CDD/PLUS, then recompile the affected modules.
- Enables multiple modules, even those written in different languages, to share one or more definitions.

The CDD/PLUS system lets developers create, analyze, and administer metadata for a software development project. Metadata is data that both describes data and defines how the data is used.

The actual data values are stored and maintained outside of the data dictionary in DEC/CMS libraries or in a data base management system. The metadata in VAX CDD/PLUS keeps track of the location, type, format, size, change history, and use of the data. The dictionary controls all changes to the metadata. Thus, a developer can manage information and application resources more effectively by allowing shared and controlled access to all metadata (usually fields and records) and by auditing the dictionary's use.

For more information on VAX CDD/PLUS, see the *VAX CDD/Plus Common Dictionary Operator User's Guide* and the *VAX CDD/Plus Common Dictionary Operator Reference Manual.* For more information about using VAX CDD/PLUS with VAX languages, see the documentation for the particular language.

2.1.10 The VMS Debugger

Digital engineers use the VMS Debugger software to observe and debug a program as it executes and to manipulate the program interactively. By issuing debugger commands at the terminal, engineers can carry out the following tasks:

- Start, stop, and resume the execution of the program
- Trace the execution path of the program
- Monitor selected locations, variables, or events
- Examine and modify the contents of variables or force events to occur
- In some cases, test the effect of modifications without having to edit the source code, recompile, and relink the program

Programming Language Support

The VMS Debugger works with the following VAX languages: Ada, BASIC, Bliss–32, C, COBOL, DIBOL, FORTRAN, MACRO–32, Pascal, PL/I, RPG, and VAX SCAN. The Debugger recognizes the syntax, expressions, data typing, and other constructs of a given language. If a program is written in more than one language, the user can change from one to another during the debugging session.

Symbolic Debugging

The VMS Debugger is a symbolic debugger. Program locations can be referenced by the symbolic names used for them in the program (the names of variables, routines, labels, and so on). It is not necessary to use virtual addresses to refer to memory locations.

Support for All Data Types

The Debugger understands all language data types, such as integer, floating point, enumeration, record, and array. It displays program variables according to their declared type.

Flexible Data Format

The VMS Debugger permits a variety of data forms and types for entry and display. By default, the source language of the program determines the format used for the entry and display of data. Other formats can be specified. For example, the contents of a program location can be entered or displayed in ASCII, hexadecimal, octal, or decimal notation.

Starting and Resuming Program Execution

The GO and STEP commands start and resume program execution. The GO command causes the program to execute until a breakpoint is reached, a watchpoint is modified, an exception condition occurs, or the program terminates. The STEP command executes a specified number of lines or instructions, or up to the next instruction of a specified class.

Breakpoints

The SET BREAK command suspends program execution at specified locations so the developer can check the current status of the program. Rather than specify a location, you can also suspend execution on certain classes of instructions, on every source line, or on certain types of events, such as exceptions and Ada tasking events.

Tracepoints

The SET TRACE command monitors the path of program execution through specific locations. When a tracepoint is triggered, the VMS Debugger reports that the tracepoint was reached and then continues execution. As with the SET BREAK command, you can also trace through classes of instructions and monitor events.

Watchpoints

The SET WATCH command causes execution to stop whenever a particular variable or other memory area has been modified. When a watchpoint is triggered, the VMS Debugger suspends execution at that point and reports the old and new values of the variable.

Manipulation of Variables and Program Locations

The EXAMINE command lets the engineer determine the value of a variable or program location. The DEPOSIT command lets the engineer change that value and then continue execution to see the effect of the change, without having to recompile, relink, and rerun the program.

Evaluation of Expressions

The EVALUATE command computes the value of a source language expression or an address expression. You can specify expressions and operators in the syntax of the language to which the VMS Debugger is currently set.

Control Structures

Logical control structures (FOR, IF, REPEAT, WHILE) can be used in commands to control the execution of other commands.

Shareable Image Debugging

You can debug shareable images (images that are not directly executable). The SET IMAGE command references the symbols declared in a shareable image.

Terminal Support

The VMS Debugger supports all of Digital's VT-series terminals and MicroVAX workstations. It uses multiple windows on the terminal screen to display extensive program state information. With this information developers can find program bugs rapidly and efficiently.

For more information on the VMS debugger, see the *VMS Debugger Manual*.

2.2 Management and Communications Tools

Many of the problems encountered in developing large and complex software projects are associated with managing all of the tasks in the process and making certain all members of the development team have the same timely information. This section discusses the following management and communications tools used at Digital:

* VAX Software Project Manager
* VAX/VMS Mail Utility
* VAX Notes

2.2.1 VAX Software Project Manager

From the earliest stages of a project, the development team needs to be able to monitor schedules, budgets, and staff requirements. Teams at Digital use the VAX Software Project Manager project management system to generate project schedules and simplify the process of estimating, planning, and controlling software development projects. The VAX Software Project Manager has the following capabilities:

* Manipulates data required to manage software projects that have up to 5000 tasks and require up to 20 different resources.

* Supports three styles of interaction: menu mode, a command-line mode, and a callable interface. All VAX Software Project Manager functions can be carried out using either the menu mode or the command-line mode. The callable interface provides a read-only mechanism for extracting project data for use outside the VAX Software Project Manager system.

VAX Software Project Manager supports an extensive collection of project-related data. Developers can enter, manipulate, and view varying amounts of data depending on the amount and depth of scheduling and reporting information needed on their project. Table 2–1 summarizes the types of data supported by VAX Software Project Manager.

Table 2–1: Data Types Supported by VAX Software Project Manager

Data Type	Description
Tasks	Individual tasks required to satisfy project objectives and product specifications
Milestones	Critical points in time
Resources	Personnel, equipment, supplies, and other materials used to carry out tasks
Schedules	Dates and resources assigned to carry out tasks
Calendar	Calendar against which to schedule
Estimation hierarchy	A tree-structured model, composed of estimation nodes that contain cost and effort estimates for the project
Software work breakdown structure	A tree-structured model of project tasks used for detailed planning
Precedence network	A chronological map of a project showing dependencies among tasks and milestones
User preference data	Optional ways to specify how VAX Software Project Manager displays its information
Access control lists	A list of accounts that can access and change project data

VAX Software Project Manager provides a powerful set of tools to help developers efficiently manipulate the project data. These tools include estimating, planning, control, and operational environment facilities.

Estimation Facility

The estimation facility allows the team to generate project schedules based on a range of assumptions about the amount and quality of available resources. This "what if" analysis can help development teams consider major trade-offs before committing to a project schedule.

The estimation facility is based on the widely accepted COCOMO (Constructive Cost Model) estimation model developed by Dr. Barry Boehm.[1] It uses algorithms that need as input the number of lines of code for the project. The facility allows the user to specify "cost drivers" that can push estimates for the project higher or lower; for example, programmer skills, product complexity, the programming environment, and so on.

Planning Facility

The planning facility generates task-level schedules. The schedules are more detailed than those of the estimation facility because more is known about the software project. Both the estimation and planning facilities allow the project manager to perform interactive "what if" analysis confidently at varying levels of detail. Additionally, the planning facility produces a project plan that can serve as a baseline against which to compare actual progress.

Control Facility

The control facility helps project leaders monitor and report project progress and costs, anticipate potential problem areas, and ensure the efficient use of all resources by comparing the progress of the project against the project plan.

Operational Environment Facility

The operational environment facility provides the means to control the environment in which VAX Software Project Manager operates; specifically, which project data base to use, who can use the system, and what each person can read and write in the project data base. Other tools in this facility allow the user to specify the resources a project has, their capabilities, their associated costs, and their availability at different times.

For more information on the VAX Software Project Manager, see the *Guide to VAX Software Project Manager*.

---

[1] Barry Boehm, *Software Engineering Economics*. Prentice-Hall: Englewood Cliffs, New Jersey, 1981.

2.2.2 The VAX/VMS Mail Utility

A communications tool that is widely used by Digital's development teams is the VAX/VMS Mail Utility (MAIL). Team members use MAIL to send electronic messages to other people on the system or any other computer that is connected to the system by means of the DECnet–VAX networking software. VAX/VMS Mail can make communications almost instantaneous. For many Digital engineers, MAIL often replaces the telephone.

For more information on MAIL, see the *VMS Mail Utility Manual*.

2.2.3 VAX Notes

Throughout the software development process development team members need to collect information for product requirements, design, and development, as well as to exchange general project information. At Digital, development teams make extensive use of the VAX Notes computer conferencing system. The VAX Notes system enables team members to conduct conferences on line, thereby reducing or eliminating much of the time and expense required to arrange and attend meetings. VAX Notes conferences can also provide a faster alternative to reviewing project documents in hard-copy format. The capability of VAX Notes to organize information can also simplify the process of including review comments in final documents.

VAX Notes is organized into "topics," in which a written "note" starts the discussion of each topic. Members of the conference can create new topics at any time and they can reply to existing notes and other people's replies. All information is stored on line and is easily examined from any node in the user's computer network. Some of the features of VAX Notes include:

- Distributed Access. Notes conferences can reside on and be accessed from any VMS system on which VAX Notes has been installed. Team members do not need an account on the system where the conference resides in order to participate.

- Moderator Support. A moderator is the person responsible for managing a conference. The moderator can restrict access to a specific group of participants by specifying names and network locations. VAX Notes allows both moderated and unmoderated conferences.

- Simple Conference Structure. VAX Notes uses numbered topics and replies to maintain the discussions in a conference, so there is no difficult hierarchy to navigate. Participants can choose topics and replies they want to read at any time.

- Use of Existing Text. Participants can create text outside of VAX Notes and then add the text to the Notes conference.

For more information on VAX Notes, see the *Guide to VAX Notes*.

2.3 Documentation Tools

A successful software product must have high-quality documentation. This includes both project documents, such as product specifications and design documents; and user documents, such as user manuals and installation guides. This section describes the following documentation tools used by development teams at Digital:

- VAX DIGITAL Standard Runoff
- VAX DOCUMENT
- DECwrite

2.3.1 VAX DIGITAL Standard Runoff

The VAX DIGITAL Standard Runoff (DSR) text-formatting utility helps developers create and maintain the extensive documentation necessary to support a development effort. The DSR command set supports documents as simple as a form letter or as complex as a multichapter manual.

The input to DSR is a file containing the text of the document and the DSR formatting codes. The output file is the formatted document that can be printed. After DSR has run, the original file remains available for further editing.

DSR has commands for a range of formatting needs, including the following basic elements:

- Pages
- Titles
- Section headers
- Graphics, lists, and notes
- Indexes and tables of contents

For more information on DSR, see the *VAX DIGITAL Standard Runoff Reference Manual*.

2.3.2 VAX DOCUMENT

Digital's development teams use the VAX DOCUMENT batch document composition system to create project documentation, such as product specifications and other design documents, and the software user documentation to support the product. VAX DOCUMENT has facilities to create, maintain, revise, format, and print complex technical documents.

The VAX DOCUMENT system produces high-quality output on a range of Digital laser printers. Many different fonts are available for all of these printers in a variety of point sizes and weights, including italic, boldface, medium, and bold italic. Thus, documents prepared with VAX DOCUMENT look typeset.

To use VAX DOCUMENT, the user creates and edits an ASCII file in which text and markup instructions are entered. The markup instructions contain no specific device or format information. Instead, they identify the text elements (such as headings, bulleted lists, or tables) that define the structure of the document. A separate file, referenced by DOCUMENT when it processes the text file, defines the typographic style of the document and its elements.

Writing a file using VAX DOCUMENT has several advantages:

- The writer can concentrate on the content of the information rather than the format.

- The final appearance of the document can be changed easily without changing the marked-up file. The marked-up file is simply reprocessed, referencing a design file that will produce a different design. For example, one design file might produce output in two-column format and another design file might produce output that spans the full width of the page.
- The documents that are produced have a consistent format.

Technical documentation for customers typically requires graphic illustrations to support text discussions. VAX DOCUMENT allows a writer to merge computer-generated graphic files into the final output document. Different tools can be used to create the graphic files as long as the files are encoded in the correct protocol for the device. DOCUMENT accepts sixel-encoded graphic files for Digital's LN03 and LN03–PLUS laser printers. It also accepts POSTSCRIPT-encoded graphic files for Digital's LN03R ScriptPrinter and PrintServer 40 laser printers.

VAX DOCUMENT also provides files that define the typographic style of several types of documents:

- Letters
- Overhead transparencies and 35mm slides
- Articles
- User manuals with software-specific information
- Military specifications
- General-purpose documents

The VAX Language-Sensitive Editor supports VAX DOCUMENT. The source files can be stored in a DEC/CMS library.

The user can specify output from VAX DOCUMENT to be printed or displayed on any Digital character-cell terminal and monospaced line printer. The user can also specify printing on the following Digital laser printers: LN03, LN03–PLUS, LN03R ScriptPrinter, and PrintServer 40. These printers produce very high-quality text and graphics output.

For more information on VAX DOCUMENT, see the *VAX DOCUMENT User Manual, Volume 1*, the *VAX DOCUMENT User Manual, Volume 2*, and *Step-by-Step: Writing with VAX DOCUMENT*.

2.3.3 DECwrite

Another documentation tool that is useful to Digital's development teams is the DECwrite new-generation WYSIWYG (What You See Is What You Get) information processing tool. DECwrite allows the user to create, edit, format, store, interchange, compose, and chart information in documents. DECwrite features a bitmapped display that shows text, graphics, and images in correct relative size and position as they will appear on output to PostScript printers. It is designed for the DECwindows environment. (DECwindows is an easily learned graphic user interface that stays consistent across a wide range of Digital desktop devices. See Section 4.4.2 for more information.)

DECwrite is a page-oriented application, which makes it attractive to team members who need to create layout-intensive documents such as product brochures. It is also a document-oriented application, so team members use it for structured documents such as proposals and specifications. DECwrite allows multiple files to be stored under one document name, thereby automatically creating a document with multiple sections or chapters. In batch mode, it can generate an index and a table of contents with separate sections for figures and tables.

DECwrite has a basic graphics editor for drawing lines, rectangles, squares, ellipses, circles, arcs, polylines, and freehand strokes. Any of these shapes can be drawn with different line weights and styles and can be filled with a variety of patterns. Once drawn, graphics objects can be modified, moved, copied, scaled, aligned relative to one another, grouped, or deleted. These graphics objects can be placed anywhere on a document page and can overlap text on the page.

DECwrite also accepts bitmapped images from scanners, paint programs, or screen capture facilities, all of which can be included in documents. These images may be cropped and scaled to fit a specific region of a page.

2.4 VMS Utilities

The VMS operating system has many powerful program development utilities. This section describes some of the most widely used, including:

The Message Utility
The Command Definition Utility
The VMS Run-Time Library
The VAX C Run-Time Library

2.4.1 The Message Utility

The Message Utility is used to construct informational, warning, or error messages in standard VMS format. Messages can indicate other conditions, for example, that a routine has run successfully or that a default value has been assigned.

Developers create a source file that specifies the information used in messages, message codes, and message symbols. Then they compile the message source file with the MESSAGE command and link the resulting object module with their facility object module. When a program is run, the Put Message ($PUTMSG) system service finds the information to use in the message by using a message argument vector.

The message argument vector includes the message code, which is a 32-bit value that uniquely identifies the message. Developers can refer to the message code in programs by means of a global symbol called the message symbol, which is also defined by information from the message source file.

The message source file consists of message definition statements and directives that define the message text, the message code values, and the message symbol. The various elements that can be included in a message source file are the following:

- Facility directive
- Severity directive
- Base message number directive
- Message definition
- Literal directive

- Identification directive
- Listing directive
- End directive

After the message file is compiled, the message object module must be linked with the facility object module (created when the source file was compiled) to produce one executable image file.

For more information on the Message Utility, see the *VMS Message Utility Manual* and the *Guide to VMS Programming Resources*.

2.4.2 The Command Definition Utility

The Command Definition Utility (CDU) software creates, deletes, or changes command definitions in a command table. CDU invokes a program when the user enters a unique Digital Command Language (DCL) command. As input, the CDU accepts a command table or a file that contains command definitions. The CDU processes this input to create a new command table in the form of executable code or an object module.

The CDU provides a way to define command-line syntax. The command table is used by the command-line interpreter (CLI) to parse commands. The CLI's parser is callable from the VAX Common Language Environment.

For more information on command definition, see the *VMS Command Definition Utility Manual* and the *Guide to VMS Programming Resources*.

2.4.3 The VMS Run-Time Library

The VMS Run-Time Library (RTL) contains two types of procedures:

- General-purpose procedures
- Language-support procedures

The general-purpose procedures are intended to be called explicitly from programs to perform common operations. The language-support procedures are intended to be called implicitly by compiler-generated code.

The general-purpose procedures in the RTL follow the VAX Procedure Calling and Condition Handling Standard (see Section 4.6.1) and the VAX/VMS Modular Programming Standard (see Section 4.6.2).

The RTL provides the following features and capabilities:

- The resource allocating procedures of the RTL provide a central repository for process resources such as virtual memory and event flags.

- Because many of the procedures are shared, they take up less space in memory.

- When new versions of the RTL are installed, engineers do not need to revise the calling program and generally do not need to relink.

The RTL contains several facilities that are groups of procedures that perform related operations. Table 2–2 lists the RTL facilities.

The general-purpose routines use explicit procedure or function calls. The following list briefly describes the types of general-purpose routines:

DECtalk Routines

These routines are used to control Digital's DECtalk devices. DECtalk is a voice synthesizer that converts computer alphanumeric text into human-quality speech. DECtalk speaks this data through its own internal speakers, an external audio system, or over a telephone.

General Utility Routines

These routines obtain records from devices, manipulate strings, convert data types for I/O, allocate resources, obtain system information, signal exceptions, establish condition handlers, enable detection of hardware exceptions, and process cross-reference data. Frequently used string-handling procedures have both JSB and CALL entry points.

Mathematical Routines

Mathematical routines perform common arithmetic, algebraic, and trigonometric functions. Frequently used mathematical routines have both JSB and CALL entry points.

Table 2–2: VMS Run-Time Library Facilities

Facility	Description
General-Purpose Routines	
DTK$	DECtalk routines
LIB$	General utility routines
MTH$	Mathematical routines
PPL$	Parallel processing routines
SMG$	Screen management routines
STR$	String manipulation routines
Language-Support Procedures	
OTS$	Language-independent support routines
BAS$	BASIC-specific support routines
COB$	COBOL-specific support routines
FOR$	FORTRAN-specific support routines
PAS$	Pascal-specific support routines
PLI$	PL/I-specific support routines
RPG$	RPG-specific support routines

Resource Allocation Routines

Resource allocation routines allocate and deallocate virtual memory, VMS local event flag numbers, BASIC and FORTRAN logical unit numbers, and dynamic strings.

Screen Management Routines

Screen management routines perform terminal-independent screen management functions. These routines help developers design, compose, and track complex images on a video screen. For more information on the screen management routines, see the *VMS RTL Screen Management (SMG$) Manual*.

Parallel Processing Routines

These routines simplify subprocess creation, interprocess communication, and resource sharing for parallel applications.

Signaling and Condition-Handling Routines

These routines perform operations that entail handling exception conditions, such as signaling exceptions, establishing condition handlers, and enabling the detection of hardware exceptions.

Syntax Analysis Routines

Syntax analysis routines analyze the syntax of strings. The library includes a table-driven parser called LIB$TPARSE and a procedure called LIB$LOOKUP_KEY that recognizes keywords.

Cross-Reference Routines

The cross-reference routines accept cross-reference data, summarize it, and format it for output. Programs access the cross-reference routines through a set of control blocks and format definition tables.

Language-Independent Support Routines

Language support routines are intended to be called implicitly by language compilers and compiled code. Compiler-generated code uses these routines to do specific tasks such as data-type conversions.

Language-Specific Support Facilities

The language-specific routines provide features such as compiled code support, file processing, format processing, error processing, and I/O processing.

For more information on the RTL routines, see the *VMS Run-Time Library Routines Volume*.

2.4.4 VAX C Run-Time Library

The primary purpose of the VAX C Run-Time Library is to allow C programs to perform I/O operations; the C language itself has no facilities for reading and writing information. The VAX C RTL also provides a means to perform many other tasks. The functions and macros supported by the VAX C RTL are as follows:

- Standard I/O functions and macros
- Terminal functions and macros
- Character-handling functions and macros

- String- and list-handling functions and macros
- Mathematical functions
- Signal functions
- Memory allocation functions
- Subprocess functions
- System functions
- Cursor Screen Management functions and macros

For more information on the VAX C Run-Time Library, refer to the *VAX C Run-Time Library Reference Manual*.

2.5 Summary of Software Development Tools

Here is a brief summary of the software development tools discussed in this chapter:

VAX Language-Sensitive Editor

Simplifies programming in any VAX language by providing multi-window, screen-oriented functions specifically designed for program development and maintenance.

VAX Source Code Analyzer

Helps software engineers understand the complexities of a large software project by allowing them to make inquiries about the symbols used in the project's code.

VAX DEC/Test Manager

Automates regression testing of software under development by executing user-supplied test data and automatically comparing the results with the expected test results.

VAX Performance and Coverage Analyzer

Analyzes the run-time behavior of software under development by performing test coverage analysis, which measures the parts of a user program executed or not executed by a given set of test data.

VAX DEC/Code Management System

Acts as the library system for storing, managing, and recording valuable information about the project files.

VAX DEC/Module Management System

Helps manage the building of application systems from component modules by determining which modules need to be recompiled after modifications and performing the appropriate actions to ensure that the software system is compiled and linked with the latest changes.

VAX SCAN

Helps software development teams create their own text-processing tools. It provides complex pattern-matching programming functions.

VAX CDD/PLUS

Makes it easier for software engineers to set up and maintain data definitions.

VMS Debugger

Provides interactive functions for debugging software.

VAX Software Project Manager

Simplifies planning and organization of medium-to-large development projects by generating schedules to track and manage project tasks.

VAX/VMS Mail Utility

Lets team members send electronic messages to other people on the system or any other computer that is connected to the system by means of the DECnet–VAX networking software.

VAX Notes

Enables the development team to create and access online conferences or meetings, thus reducing the need to travel and coordinate schedules.

VAX DIGITAL Standard Runoff

Provides text-formatting functions for text editors.

VAX DOCUMENT

Provides tools for text creation, text and graphics integration, sophisticated document formatting, and typeset-quality output on laser printers.

DECwrite

Enables developers to create, edit, format, store, interchange, compose, and chart information in their documents. Features a bitmapped display and is designed for the DECwindows environment.

Message Utility

Enables the software development team to construct informational, warning, or error messages to be used by the software application.

Command Definition Utility

Used to create, delete, or change command definitions in a command table.

VMS Run-Time Library

Provides a series of procedures designed to be called from programs to perform common operations.

Chapter 3

Project Management

Project management is the process of coordinating the several inter-related tasks of developing a product and bringing it to market. As project teams develop larger and more complex applications, managing the life cycle becomes more difficult and more time-consuming. Good project management is therefore vital to the success of a software development project.

This chapter discusses some of the key concepts in project management. The chapter is divided into three main topics:

- Development projects and teams
- Project planning and control
- Project documentation

3.1 Development Projects and Teams

Digital relies on product teams to develop and deliver products. This approach recognizes that bringing a new product to market on time and within budget requires cooperation and shared decision-making.

3.1.1 Product Team

Every product-development effort requires the interaction of manage-ment, marketing, engineering, customer services, sales, manufacturing, and finance. Generally, these team members are first brought together by the product and marketing managers.

Figure 3–1 shows the interactions among members of a typical product team.

Figure 3–1: Product Team Interactions

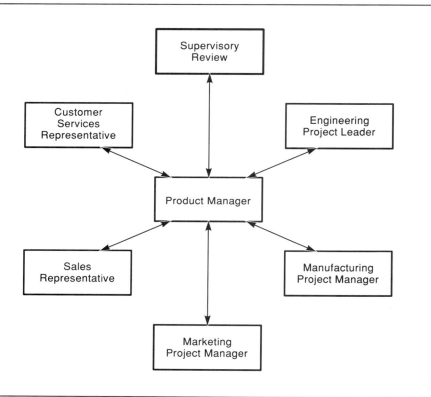

The product team shares these responsibilities:

- Monitoring development progress against the business plan
- Ensuring that software developers understand the user's perspective

- Evaluating prototypes for functionality
- Continuously reviewing product plans and documenting changes

The product team resolves all issues that arise while carrying out these responsibilities.

3.1.2 Development Team

The team within a software engineering organization responsible for delivering the product is generally called the project or development team. Figure 3–2 shows typical development team members.

Figure 3–2: Development Team Members

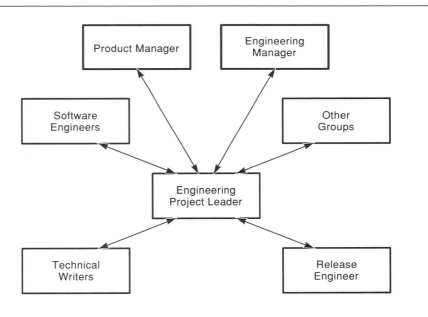

An engineering project leader directs the daily engineering activities of the development team and represents its interests on the product team. Members of this team include one or more software engineers, technical writers, release engineers, field test administrators, software manufacturing planners, and administrative personnel.

The success of a project lies in the effectiveness of the team. One measure of effectiveness is the communication among team members. At Digital, the primary communications tools are meetings, reports, and electronic dialogue (MAIL and VAX Notes). Another measure of effectiveness is the ability of all individuals to manage their tasks on the project, as described in the next sections.

3.1.2.1 Responsibilities of the Engineering Project Leader

The engineering project leader plays a central role in product development. He or she is responsible for the following:

- **Coordinating the daily engineering activities required to meet the criteria for each phase of development**. To meet this responsibility, the engineering project leader:
  — Plans projects
  — Manages activities
  — Evaluates status
  — Manages change
- **Ensuring that the engineering plan is consistent with the support plans of the product development team and that all support plans receive the necessary engineering attention**. To meet this responsibility, the engineering project leader:
  — Participates in product development team meetings
  — Conducts regular team meetings with the development team members
  — Reviews and approves all team documents
  — Submits status reports
  — Identifies and manages items that change the scope of the project

- **Keeping engineering management fully informed of project developments**. To meet this responsibility, the engineering project leader:
  - Identifies resource requirements for the project
  - Negotiates commitments for project resources
  - Reviews the performance of project team members
  - Recognizes performance problems with assigned personnel and notifies the appropriate managers
  - Submits regular status reports
- **Building an effective development team.** To meet this responsibility, the engineering project leader:
  - Directs and coordinates all resources on project tasks
  - Assigns individual team members to complete each task
  - Analyzes necessary trade-offs required to respond to changes in the needs of the project
  - Provides a regular forum to communicate project status and accomplishments
  - Manages changes and suggestions from the team
  - Manages dependencies with other resources on the project
  - Identifies dependencies that affect the start and completion of each task
  - Estimates the time and effort needed to complete each task and schedule start and completion dates
  - Specifies the criteria that will indicate that a particular task is complete
  - Sets priorities and identifies potential risks and conflicts

3.1.2.2 Responsibilities of Development Team Members

Each team member develops a specific portion of the product. As a group, they also review the work of their fellow team members to ensure the cohesion of their efforts. Working with the project leader, team members are responsible for:

- **Planning their tasks to ensure efficient budgeting of time and resources.** To meet this responsibility, team members:
  - Make sure their tasks are clearly defined

- Understand how much time each task requires and ensure that time is available for all task commitments
- Confer with the project leader if they need help in planning their tasks or in redefining tasks that are not properly defined

- **Maintaining a list of their tasks and tracking their progress against the planned schedule.**
- **Working on tasks according to the development schedule.** To meet this responsibility, team members bring difficult problems to the attention of their project leader promptly. Table 3–1 lists several common types of problems and courses of action to follow.

Table 3–1: Responses to Common Task-Related Problems

Type of Problem	Response
Improperly defined task	Discuss problem with project leader immediately. No matter how much time is spent planning, new information may cause changes in a task, priority, or content.
Missing task	Discuss problem with project leader immediately.
Prerequisite not met	The project leader may need to alter priorities of other tasks to allow a task to begin, or defer a task at that point and start another task.
Revision required after the task is complete	Do not wait until the last minute to check if the task is complete. Discuss progress with others at status review meetings as well as with the project leader. The impact of rework is generally underestimated.

3.1.2.3 Progress Reports and Team Meetings

Regular progress reports facilitate communication between team members and the project leader and provide the project leader with information needed to manage the project.

Progress reports include the following information:

- Tasks or components worked on
- Time spent on each task
- Time remaining on all tasks
- Tasks completed

Progress reports are the key topic at team meetings, which are typically held once a week. During the meeting, the project leader identifies the accomplishments and problems from the previous week and sets goals for the upcoming week. This information, collected weekly, can contribute to a monthly project report.

Team meetings are most useful when everyone is prepared and ready to participate actively. Team members should be able to discuss their current status and their plans for the next two to four weeks. Thus, everyone is made aware of what the others are doing.

3.2 Project Planning and Control

The purpose of project planning is to carry a project through all phases of development on time and within budget while meeting all technical objectives. Effective project planning entails the following key activities:

- Identifying the project tasks
- Identifying the resources necessary to carry out the project tasks
- Organizing the tasks and resources to meet project objectives

Although most of the planning occurs when the preliminary and final engineering plans are prepared, in reality the project plan is continuously updated to reflect the project's evolution.

3.2.1 Project Schedule

During preliminary planning, the development team prepares a project schedule. The schedule depends on many factors:

- The resources available for the project (people, equipment, and so on)
- Dependencies on other projects

- Marketing needs
- Special field testing requirements

The following checklist contains tasks and other items to consider when allocating time for the schedule:

- **Project Work**
  - Producing prototypes
  - Supporting prototypes
  - Testing
  - Responding to reported problems with the software
  - Fixing errors in the code
  - Installing operating systems
  - Verifying the product on new hardware or operating systems
  - Testing performance
  - Adjusting for delays in other projects that affect the schedule
  - Reviewing documentation and code
  - Holding project meetings
  - Preparing review documents
- **Overhead**
  - Administrative work (for example, demonstrations)
  - Training
  - Presentations and business trips
  - Vacations
  - Staffing changes

Digital's development teams use the following steps to establish realistic schedules:

1. Produce a product design with enough detail to minimize risks.
2. Divide the project into units or tasks suitable for scheduling.

   The team uses the physical design of the software to divide the project into units or tasks that are easy to schedule. Note that a logical design might not directly correspond to a task that can be scheduled.

3. Estimate the time to complete tasks.

   Team members estimate the time necessary to complete their individual tasks, including overhead.

4. Determine milestones.

   Milestones are important points in the project that typically reflect significant progress in the product's development.

5. Determine critical paths, that is, the completion order and dependencies among tasks.

6. Define the actual time period in which project activities will be completed.

7. Assign people to tasks.

   The project leader makes sure that assigned parties agree with the time estimates.

8. Schedule actual working hours.

   Add time for meetings, vacations, and so on. For example, a project leader may have a task that requires four days. If 50 percent of the assigned engineer's time is taken with overhead, then the job actually will take eight days to complete. The resulting schedule consists of a series of milestones mapped to calendar dates. Figure 3–3 depicts this mapping process.

Depending on the type of project, the schedule may have to allow for a significant degree of uncertainty, particularly for projects whose requirements are not well defined. To cope with this uncertainty, the team regularly updates and reevaluates the project schedule. In effect, during much of the project, scheduling is an ongoing process.

As the project advances, however, scheduling dependencies increase between the groups represented on the project team. Furthermore, the schedule must become increasingly firm as the dates for field test and manufacturing approach.

Figure 3–3: Mapping Units to Calendar

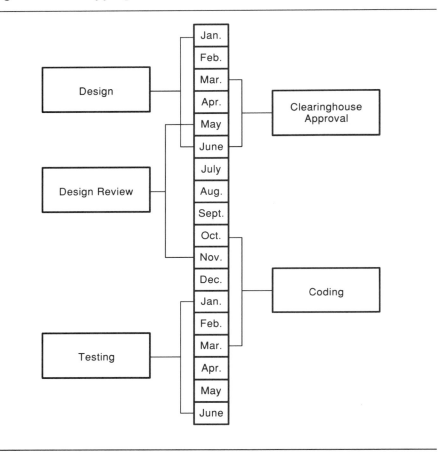

3.2.2 Project Control

To ensure a successful outcome, the development team needs a project control strategy. Digital's development teams use the following project control model, adapting it as necessary to the needs of the project. Each function is typically carried out by the project leader.

- Directing: Assigning project tasks to team members or outside groups; redirecting tasks and assigning special action items as required.
- Monitoring: Staying abreast of the progress of individual tasks and the project itself by personally observing tasks and reviewing formal and informal status reports.
- Evaluating: Comparing actual progress to the schedule; the comparison leads to decisions regarding the project or task, reviews held, and reports prepared for management.
- Replanning: Updating the project plan or task assignments.

Figure 3–4 illustrates the project control model. For simplicity, the functions in the model are represented as discrete blocks. In practice, of course, the operations may overlap.

Figure 3–4: Project Control Model

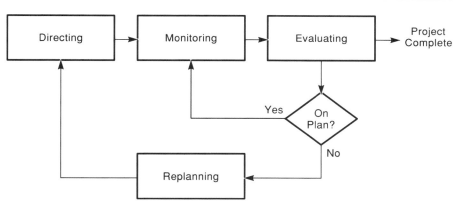

As a part of the control strategy, the engineering project leader can examine how the updated schedules deviate from original schedules. Using statistical analysis, the project leader may uncover a consistent pattern of deviation the team can use to set up future schedules. In this way, the schedule more accurately reflects the ongoing progress of the project.

3.2.3 The VAX Software Project Manager

At Digital, scheduling and task assignment are facilitated by the VAX Software Project Manager. This tool, described in Section 2.2.1, helps automate the process of mapping the scheduled tasks to a calendar and assigning the tasks to team members. The VAX Software Project Manager provides several advantages over other methods of project management:

- Quickly generates schedules, thereby making them easier to maintain; any changes or unforeseen events can be factored into new schedules.
- Communicates information to the entire development team rather than limiting access to the project leader.
- Helps prevent mechanical or mathematical errors in schedules after the team determines what units it will use.

3.3 Project Documentation

Good project documentation is essential to successful project management. This section describes a number of the project-related documents used at Digital to plan and control product development:

- Market requirements document
- Product requirements document
- Alternatives/feasibility study
- High level design document
- Detailed design document
- Product specification
- Development plan
- Field test plan
- Field test results

Figure 3–5 shows the flow of information among the various documents as related to the development phases.

Figure 3–5: Information Flow Among Phase Documents

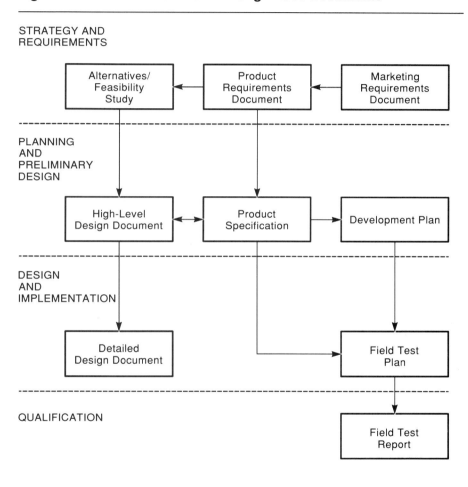

3.3.1   Marketing Requirements Document

The marketing requirements document has the following purposes:

- Demonstrates an understanding of the marketplace that this product will satisfy. It presents market requirements from the customer's perspective.
- Analyzes customer needs and describes customer priorities, international considerations, and possible trade-offs in the areas of pricing, cost of ownership, delivery, function, quality, ease-of-use, performance, compatibility, and serviceability.
- Reviews the product position compared to competitive products.

The product or marketing manager prepares the marketing requirements document during the strategy and requirements phase, with help from other marketing organizations.

3.3.2   Product Requirements Document

The product requirements document has the following purposes:

- Defines in measurable terms the goals, capabilities, and external characteristics of the product.
- Describes the requirements of the product as agreed to by the product team.
- Proposes what the final packaged product will look like to the customer.
- Describes in detail the primary product features that will be delivered to satisfy both critical market needs and success factors that were identified in the marketing requirements document.
- Defines the specific technical requirements of the product.
- Identifies the methods, tools, processes, and metrics that will be used to deliver and verify the quality of the stated features.
- Identifies international requirements.
- Identifies interdependencies.

The product manager prepares the product requirements document during the strategy and requirements phase with help from engineering, marketing, customer services, and other product and engineering groups.

3.3.3 Alternatives/Feasibility Study

The alternatives/feasibility study analyzes the trade-offs required to deliver a product that meets the conditions of the product requirements document. It quantifies the total life-cycle costs of the alternatives for meeting the requirements.

The alternatives/feasibility study has the following purposes:

- Identifies options within the company and industry that will allow development using existing company products (available concurrently or in development).

- Identifies and describes various approaches for meeting the conditions defined in the product requirements document. Focuses on methods required to acquire and integrate the product within the constraints of cost and schedule.

- Specifies the interdependencies involved in developing the product.

- Identifies alternative product and component design approaches.

- Identifies the cost requirements by phase based on the recommended schedule.

The engineering development team prepares the alternatives/feasibility study during the strategy and requirements phase.

3.3.4 Product Specification

A product specification describes in measurable terms the goals, capabilities, and external characteristics of a component software product. It is the development team's commitment to meet the product requirements.

The product specification is based on the product requirements document. Usually, it also corresponds to a reference from a system specification; that is, the document that describes the plan to deliver the total system, of which this product may be a component. Additional characteristics of the product specification include the following:

- Serves as the starting point for much of the design work for the product
- Helps identify the tasks required to create the product
- Estimates the resources needed to deliver the product
- Provides a measure against which the product is evaluated
- Serves as the source document to be used by the service organizations and by other engineering groups, both hardware and software, to plan other components of the system

3.3.5 Development Plan

The development plan serves as the master plan and schedule for successfully delivering a component software product. It is used to manage the product development effort.

The development plan has the following purposes:

- Describes the major tasks of each functional group.
- Details the commitments, schedules, and costs of all functional groups that are responsible for the product's objectives.
- Identifies when product reviews will occur in relation to the efforts of functional groups.
- Describes the development project for designing, building, testing, evaluating, and delivering the product.
- Lists the major issues and risks identified in the strategy and requirements phase that are critical to the design freeze.

The development team prepares the development plan during the planning and preliminary design phase, with help from the product manager and marketing representative.

3.3.6   High-Level Design Document

The high-level design document describes the design for the system that meets the functional requirements detailed in the product specification. The high-level design document translates the requirements of the product specification into a physical model showing how the development team will design and integrate the system components into a complete product.

In planning a software product, a Digital product team divides each system into components that represent a part of the capabilities of the product. These components provide a basis for planning, developing, and integrating the product. The high-level design of the system establishes the system interfaces and data structures and the test specification for system integration. The high-level design for each component establishes the component interfaces and data structures, processing within the component, and the test specification for component integration.

The primary audience for the high-level design document consists of design engineers who will design components of the system, review engineers who will review the designs, maintenance engineers who will support the system, and the project manager.

3.3.7   Detailed Design Document

The detailed design document translates the high-level designs into module designs and test procedures. Each module design with its associated test procedure is then used during the design and implementation phase. The detailed design also describes the procedures the development team will use for unit and integration testing of the component or system.

The detailed design document corresponds to the current version of the software. Changes to the design are reflected in changes to the design documentation.

3.3.8 Field Test Plan

The field test plan has the following purposes:

- Serves as the master plan for field testing a component software product.
- Serves as the operational plan used to track the product's testing effort.
- Describes what is to be tested during field test.
- Describes the strategy for carrying out the field test.
- Describes how the field test sites are selected.
- Describes how the field test will be evaluated.
- Describes the major tasks of each functional group.
- Details the responsibilities and schedules of internal groups and test sites during the field test.

The development team prepares the field test plan during the design and implementation phase, with help from the product manager and field test administrator.

3.3.9 Field Test Report

The field test report collects and summarizes the results from the field test. It contains information such as the following:

- A general overview of the field test. This section describes each test site and includes information such as the location of each test site, and the start date and end date of the test at each site.
- A section for each field test site. These sections contain information about how the customers used the product, including their general applications as well as actual field test use. It also describes the customers' reactions to the product.
- A problem report section. This section describes all problem reports submitted and their resolution.

The field test administrator prepares the field test report with help from the product manager and development team.

Chapter 4

Planning and Preliminary Design

After the documents of the strategy and requirements phase are written and approved, attention turns to the software engineering development team and the planning and preliminary design phase begins. During this phase, the development team, with help from the rest of the product team, determines precisely what to build and how to build it. The product specification, the development plan (schedule) and the high-level design document are prepared. When the project specifications are complete, analysis and design can then take place and the software product takes on full-system definition.

During this phase, top-level designs are prepared for all forms, data structures, program modules, file formats, and human interfaces based on the information in the product specification. The completed design gives the project technical definition. The design document makes it possible to keep the design specifications in one location, accessible to all software engineers. As the project evolves, so does the design document.

Figure 4–1 shows the relationships among the key engineering tasks and documents of this phase.

Figure 4–1: Planning and Preliminary Design Phase

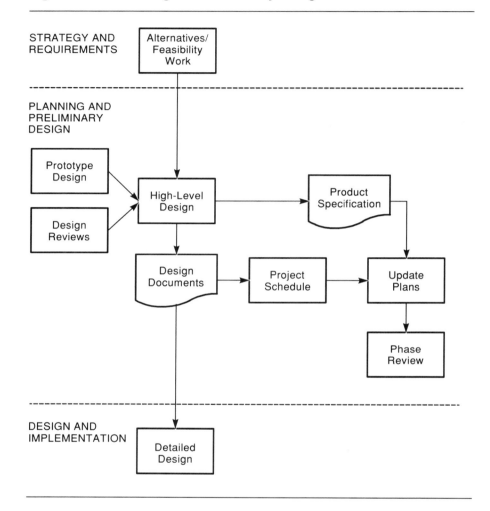

4.1 High-Level Design

The high-level design work provides information that the development team can use to prepare preliminary versions of the product specification and the development plan, including the project schedule.

The product requirements document and the alternatives and feasibility study, written in the strategy and requirements phase, form the basis for the high-level design.

4.1.1   High-Level Design Process

A Digital development team typically considers two major areas of system design:

- High-level design (sometimes called logical design or analysis) identifies the multiple components (modules) of a product. The high-level design also identifies the interactions among components, the relative size and scope of the components, and any shared components. The team provides enough detail on each design component to write the detailed designs.

- Detailed design (sometimes called physical design or implementation design) divides the product into units based on how each component will be implemented. The team provides enough detail on each design unit to allow the code to be written. Section 5.1.2 provides information on detailed design.

During high-level design, the development team begins to define the product components, design criteria, design constraints, and the functional design of each component. The functional designs specify the inputs, outputs, and processing of data. Data flow diagrams can be useful in preparing high-level designs. The finished high-level design documents include both component and systemwide test designs.

When designing an application, the Digital design team plans centralized and common functions and designs the application's system of modules to produce efficient interaction among them. The development team also attempts to create routines that are highly modular. A modular approach to design has several benefits:

- Changes to the code are made in one place in the application rather than in several places that reuse the same source code.

- The development team can write tests more easily for modular routines because their functions are carefully delimited.

- Many utilities can access other routines directly without going through functional routines.

- Tests are more likely to find code errors because some sections, for example, the common access level or entry points, would be repeatedly tested along with the functional routines. The result should be fewer errors.
- Highly modular code can be reused more easily in other applications.

Modular routines have the following characteristics:

- They have one primary function.
- They are standalone.
- They are callable.
- They contain sufficient levels of error checking to detect problems that occur during their execution.

As Figure 4–2 illustrates, a modularly designed application can be represented as a series of levels. The user interface is at the highest level, followed by the functional level, the access level, and the data base level. The functional level contains the various utilities or routines that give the application its functional capabilities. The modularity in this example enables the utilities in the functional level to use the data base through a common access level or entry point. Thus, each utility in the functional level does not need its own individual routines to access the data base. Instead, the access level has a common set of routines that all the utilities in the functional level use to access the data base.

4.1.2 High-Level Testing Analysis

High-level testing analysis refers to the testing strategy needed for the product and is a part of the high-level design. The product requirements document serves as the starting point for high-level testing analysis. For analysis, the team can use the product itself (assuming the development effort is for a new version of an existing product) or a prototype.

Figure 4–2: Modular Design Levels

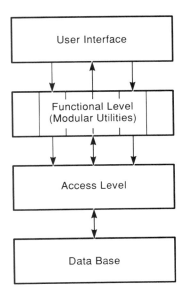

The VAX DEC/Test Manager, described in Chapter 2, is an automated regression testing tool that can serve as a resource in planning the testing strategy. See Section 2.1.4 for more information on the VAX DEC/Test Manager.

The results of testing analysis take several forms:

- Details on the test system requirements for the product specification and the development plan
- Support for the schedule estimate
- Information that becomes part of the high-level and detailed design documents

Refer to Section 7.3.1 for additional information on the relationship between design and test planning.

4.2 Design Methodologies

Designs can be communicated by means of written documents, coded and commented files, or both. Each method has a significant shortcoming. The subjectivity and lack of precision of natural language creates difficulties as the team translates the designs into highly structured, high-level coding languages. On the other hand, using a programming language to communicate a design introduces such fine detail that the true power and flexibility of design work may be lost.

Digital's solution to this problem is to use design methodologies. The various methodologies (Yourdon, Warnier and Orr, and so on) provide a rigid syntax (operators, operands), data (nouns), and a grammar that governs the relationships among the component parts of the design.

The syntax and grammar of such formal methodologies provide two major benefits:

- They provide ways to validate designs.
- They minimize the ambiguity inherent in the design medium.

When choosing a methodology, determine what is most commonly used in your own company. Learning several methodologies is not practical for the actual design process. If your group favors no particular methodology, personal preference can be the deciding factor.

See Appendix D, Additional Reading, for recommended reading on design methodologies.

4.3 Prototypes

The development team may choose to produce an operational prototype for a subset of the application to achieve some or all of the following goals:

- Demonstrate whether or not product features are feasible
- Gather data on usability and performance issues
- Communicate design and implementation ideas
- Solicit user feedback

Producing a prototype entails four steps:

1. Setting the goals for the prototype and communicating them to management.
2. Producing enough designs to make it possible to carry out the coding.
3. Choosing a programming language.
4. Writing the code.

The language chosen for the prototype is often the implementation language. However, fourth-generation languages are particularly useful for developing prototypes quickly (for example, VAX RALLY, VAX SQL, and the VAX COBOL GENERATOR).

Once the prototype is running, the team may gather statistics on its use to measure the prototype against the product's requirements. The prototype can be particularly helpful in designing the human interface. The team may also use the prototype to present information at a design review meeting.

4.4 Human Interface Design

To create a truly useful product, every development team needs to understand how and why customers will use it. Without this knowledge, the team stands little chance of creating an effective product that is easy to use.

4.4.1 Usability Issues

Advances in interface design have led users to expect systems that are easy to learn and use. Development teams need to consider how to design the system's architecture to meet those expectations. Digital's DECwindows interface, described in Section 4.4.2, has been developed to make a consistent human interface available to developers of software applications.

An experienced development team recognizes that a principal test of software quality is how easily a user can learn and use it. To pass this test, the team must anticipate the user's needs, which is not always easy to do. In developing a human interface design, the Digital development team follows the phases of the development process discussed in this book: requirements, specifications, design, and iterative implementation and testing. During each of these phases, human factors experts can help ensure that the final product meets users' needs.

4.4.1.1 Requirements

Gathering requirements is often one of the most difficult tasks in any software project. This is especially true for interface design. Typically, the team needs to learn about the users, their needs, and about competitive products. Human factors specialists can provide useful information on user requirements. The development team has an easier time if the product is similar to products that team members have used or developed, or if the users have similar experience.

Observations gathered in laboratory settings are helpful, but they reflect an artificial and limited environment that differs from the one in which customers are likely to work. By observing customers in their work environment, the development team can better understand the customer's needs.

4.4.1.2 Specifications

To design a good user interface, the development team must know what it wants to achieve and how to measure its objectives. There is no list of usability objectives that applies to every product. Usability objectives for a particular product must reflect the type of work for which it is used, users' experiences with similar products, the technology available, and the resources of the development team.

Developers can construct a usability specification table to summarize the attribute components and help the development team make trade-offs among desired levels for many of the application's attributes. Table 4–1 shows part of a generic usability specification table.

Table 4–1: Sample Usability Specification Table

Performance Attribute	Measuring Technique	Metric	Worst Case	Planned Level	Best Case	Current Level
Initial use	Benchmark task from use data, performed by practiced designer in a given time; may be harder at mastery level	Speed metric S=PC/T[1]	10%	20%	30%	1–14%
Occasional use		Speed metric	25%	50%	65%	30–40%
Mastery		Speed metric	50%	75%	90%	25–85%
Installation	Install on test system	Time to install correctly	30 min.	15 min.		

[1]Work Speed (S): P is the percent of task completed (according to a scoring scheme); C is a constant equal to the time an optimal user needs to complete the task; T is the time spent of task in minutes.

After establishing usability attributes, the team devises a technique for collecting information on user performance for each attribute. Possible techniques include the following:

- Ask the user to perform a specific task (benchmarking)
- Monitor the user during unstructured use (logging, observing)
- Interview the user
- Survey users
- Ask the user to complete a questionnaire
- Ask the user to describe critical incidents that reveal successes or failures

To measure user performance, the team needs to quantify the information it has gathered. Possible measurements include the following:

- Time required to complete a task
- Percentage of task completed
- Percentage of task completed per unit time
- Ratio of successes to failures
- Time spent resolving errors

- Percentage or number of errors
- Percentage or number of competitive products that the product is better than
- Number of commands used
- Frequency with which online help and documentation are consulted
- Time spent using online help or documentation
- Percentage of favorable and unfavorable user comments
- Number of repetitions of failed commands
- Number of runs of successes and of failures
- Number of times interface misleads users
- Number of good and bad features recalled by users
- Number of available commands not used
- Number of regressive behaviors
- Number of users who prefer the product over another
- Number of times users need to work around a problem
- Number of times users are disrupted from a work task by the product
- Number of times users lose control of the system
- Number of times users express frustration or satisfaction

For each measurement, the team also establishes what it considers a good performance, a bad performance, the level of performance it seeks, and the level that the product can deliver at a given phase in its development. The following can provide a basis for comparison:

- An existing system or previous version
- A competitive system
- Doing the task without a computer
- An absolute scale
- Other prototypes
- Users' earlier performance
- Each individual component of a system
- A successive split of the difference between best and worst values observed in user tests

While establishing user performance goals, the team also considers these questions:

- How well do the attributes reflect system usability?
- Do all team members agree on each attribute?
- Can each attribute be measured in practice?
- Are resources available to measure all the attributes?
- Are the users defined clearly enough to find representative users?

4.4.1.3 Iterative Design

Iterative design to improve usability means incremental, evolutionary, and conscious iteration. This kind of development requires early, repeated feedback from typical users. Subsets of the system are tested early in the development cycle with actual users. Throughout the development cycle, the team enhances the software in small, incremental versions that incorporate the feedback from users. Each new version improves the system's quality. Improvements are measured against the target levels of usability attributes.

4.4.2 DECwindows

The rapid evolution of the workstation market and the technological advances in workstations have created the need to change the interface design of many software products. The DECwindows architecture frees developers from many interface issues and allows them to concentrate on the functional levels of the application. The DECwindows architecture integrates the graphics programming interfaces of three operating systems: VMS, ULTRIX, and MS–DOS. The primary features of DECwindows include the following:

- A common user interface that adheres to industry-standard PC conventions
- A set of personal productivity applications (for example, electronic mail and personal data base query)
- Network-transparent windowing and communication between VAX systems, VAXmate computers, and other industry-standard PCs, using the X Window System (the industry-standard window system for graphics programming interfaces developed at MIT)

- Common application environments that use the industry-standard X Toolkit, software, and an extensible toolkit

The DECwindows architecture allows a user on any workstation, running any operating system, to use windows transparently in a networked environment. It also allows windowing programs to be transported easily.

The DECwindows programming environment provides both the standard X Toolkit and the Digital XUI Toolkit (X User Interface) with additional features.

Common User Interface

The common user interface has the following characteristics:

- Window and user-interface managers
- Programming libraries

The window and user-interface managers make it easy to display and use multiple windows on the workstation screen. They allow the user to create new windows and manipulate existing ones. Window management is common to both the VMS and ULTRIX operating systems. The use of a common style of human interface across both operating systems ensures that the users who work with both operating systems need not learn more than one interface.

Procedural interfaces or bindings define how users access run-time programming libraries from a particular language. Existing specifications for the X Window System run-time libraries have been provided by MIT; future specifications are expected from the ongoing work on X standards. These specifications include the MIT-defined Xlib and the C language bindings.

Run-time libraries provide a number of functions:

- Resource management capabilities
- Graphics and text display
- Menu and other high-level input mechanisms
- Access to input events
- Data exchange between applications or the code that executes the application

Table 4–2 lists and describes some specific run-time libraries.

Table 4–2: DECwindows Run-Time Libraries

Run-Time Library	Description
Xlib	Basic graphics and windowing code standard in the industry
X Toolkit	Industry-standard user-interface tools
XUI Toolkit	DECwindows application user interface
DEC GKS[1]	Digital's implementation of industry-standard 2D graphics library
DEC PHIGS[2]	Digital's implementation of industry-standard 3D graphics library

[1]Graphical Kernel System

[2]Programmer's Hierarchical Interactive Graphics System

Developers can use all of these libraries. For example, Xlib has the functionality to draw a line and the X Toolkit can create a primitive menu. The X Toolkit is a package of tools for programmers that extends the basic functionality provided by the X Window System to support human interface construction within user applications. It does so by providing application programmers with a common set of intrinsic routines for developing industry-standard applications. The X Toolkit library allows programmers to create menus, scroll bars, and other user-interface features.

The Digital XUI Toolkit (X User Interface) is the programmer and user interface developed by Digital for X-based workstations. It provides additional routines for creating complex applications based on the X Window System. It defines the style, behavior, and human interface applications. In addition, it provides for resource management and internationalization. The XUI Toolkit makes it easier to write applications with consistent qualities. Its industry-standard libraries ensure compatibility with industry standards such as GKS and PHIGS.

DEC GKS (Graphical Kernel System) is the graphics library for programming applications requiring the generation of 2D pictures with large amounts of data. It is best suited for generating static pictures such as complex charts and graphs. DEC GKS provides a rich set of input and output graphics functions as well as device independence. Applications written in DEC GKS are portable between device and operating systems.

DEC PHIGS (Programmer's Hierarchical Interactive Graphics System) is a graphics subroutine library for applications requiring interactive, real-time editing of 3D dynamic pictures with realistic appearance. It offers a variety of high-level primitives for creating graphics elements, including advanced lighting, shading, and depth cueing primitives, powerful ways to control the hierarchy and relation of graphics data. Applications written in DEC PHIGS are portable between device and operating systems.

Network Transparency

The DECwindows architecture provides a common network-transparent application environment that is based on the X Window System.

An application developed for the DECwindows environment runs on a VAX computer using either the VMS or ULTRIX operating system, and directs its input and output to a DECstation or VAXstation workstation. Because both the VMS and ULTRIX operating systems understand the X communications protocol, both can run the same applications.

The application is local if the input and output occur on the same workstation that is executing the application. Requests of the application are translated on the local processor to manipulate the hardware through the local processor's device drivers. The application is remote if input and output from the application occur over the network (for example, if the application runs on a VAX 8800 in a computer laboratory while users manipulate that application from workstations in their offices). For the remote applications, requests are transported over the network using the X protocol. On the remote node, a server translates the application requests and then manipulates the hardware through that node's local device drivers.

The DECwindows architecture also supports the integration of industry-standard PCs into Digital's computing environment. VAX system-based applications written for the DECwindows environment can use networked PCs as a windowed display device. The PC receives the X protocol requests and serves as the user interface for the VAX application; the PC maps the wire protocol packets onto PC calls to support the remote application display. Thus, users can run local

PC applications outside the DECwindows environment and also have access to VAX system-based applications in the network.

4.5 Design Reviews

The purpose of design reviews is to find and correct design errors as early as possible (see Figure 4–3). For a typical review, one team member distributes a design document to the rest of the team. After reviewing the document, the team holds a review meeting at which the team member most closely involved with the design might make a formal presentation. During the meeting, the other team members may question particular features of the design. Ultimately, the group decides whether to use the design or to change it.

Design reviews also help engineers become familiar with parts of the project they may not know; however, design reviews are not meant to carry out design work itself. If the product is to be marketed internationally, the design is reviewed in the context of the worldwide requirements for the product.

The design review process is informal. Adopt a process that the entire development team can work with. Design documents may undergo peer review, either during periodic project meetings or between an engineer and the project leader.

4.5.1 Design Review Guidelines

The following questions are answered during the design review:

1. Does the design help to meet at least one project goal?
2. Does the design implement any unnecessary functions?
3. Does the design identify all side effects and changed values?
4. Does the design properly address all human factors?
5. Is the design complete?
6. Is the design easy to understand and unambiguous?

Figure 4–3: Design Review Process

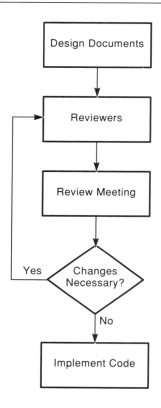

7. Is the design self-contained? Could someone new to the project successfully implement the project from the documentation alone?
8. Does the design show links among all applicable modules?
9. Does the design list all external dependencies?
10. Does the design consider packaging and installation requirements?
11. Does the design list all applicable control blocks, tables, data structures, and all new functions for which they are used?
12. Does the design identify all new macros, symbols, and coding conventions?

13. Does the design identify all specific values required and set?

14. Is the design written at an appropriate and consistent level of detail?

15. Does the design address all known possible cases?

16. Does the design address all exception cases?

17. Does the design address abnormal cases and error conditions?

18. Does the design address all appropriate operating environments and devices?

19. Does the design provide for new logic and function that is consistent with existing logic and function?

20. Are all fields described correctly? Are any of the fields missing?

21. Should an external routine be used rather than performing the function internally?

22. Does the module provide for all possible input parameters?

23. Does the module process and pass all parameters correctly?

24. Are all return codes, parameter formats, and so on correctly identified? Alternatively, does the design document reference their definitions adequately?

25. Are all issues of code protection addressed?

26. Does the design provide for reentrance or reusability?

27. Have performance issues been addressed?

28. Has storage size been addressed?

29. Does the function use existing facilities whenever possible?

30. Are there any paging or swapping issues?

31. Have the following issues been addressed:
    — Maintainability
    — Reliability
    — Evolvability
    — Functionality
    — Compatibility
    — User documentation
    — User training
    — Software specialist training

4.6 Standards

In the emerging environment of industry standards, developers need to
be familiar with the standards that are relevant to their own areas of
software development. Standards come from a number of sources. The
following sections introduce important software standards:

- For coding VMS applications:
  - The VAX Procedure Calling and Condition Handling Standard
  - The VAX/VMS Modular Programming Standard
- For migrating to open standards:
  - IEEE standards
  - International standards

4.6.1 The VAX Procedure Calling and Condition Handling Standard

The VAX Procedure Calling and Condition Handling Standard describes
the techniques used by all VAX languages for invoking routines and
passing data between them. By default, these conventions are followed
by all program calls in Digital's programming languages and other
layered products. The standard specifies the following attributes:

- Register use
- Stack use
- Function value return
- Argument list

The VAX Procedure Calling and Condition Handling Standard also
defines such attributes as the calling sequence, the argument data
types and descriptor formats, condition handling, and stack unwinding.
The *VMS Utility Routines Manual* discusses these additional attributes
in detail.

Register and Stack Use

The VAX Procedure Calling and Condition Handling Standard defines several registers and their uses, as listed in Table 4–3.

Table 4–3: VAX Register Use

Register	Use
PC	Program counter
SP	Stack pointer
FP	Current stack frame pointer
AP	Argument pointer
R1	Environment value (when necessary)
R0, R1	Function value return registers

Any called routine can use registers R2 through R11 for computation, and the AP register as a temporary register.

Function Value Return

A function is a routine that returns a single value to the calling routine. The function value represents the return value that is assigned to the function's identifier during execution. According to the VAX Procedure Calling and Condition Handling Standard, a function value may be returned either as an actual value or a condition value that indicates success or failure.

Argument List

The VAX Procedure Calling and Condition Handling Standard also defines a data structure called the argument list. Engineers use an argument list to pass information to a routine and receive results. An argument list is a collection of longwords in memory that represents a routine parameter list and possibly includes a function value.

4.6.2 VAX/VMS Modular Programming Standard

The VAX/VMS Modular Programming Standard sets the minimum criteria necessary to ensure the correct interface at the procedure level between a team's software and software written by others. The *Guide to Creating VMS Modular Procedures* contains full details on the VAX/VMS Modular Programming Standard.

Scope of Standard

The VAX/VMS Modular Programming Standard gives engineers a common environment in which to write code. If all engineers coding VMS applications follow this standard, any modular procedure added to a procedure library will not conflict with procedures currently in the library or with procedures that might be added in the future.

The elements of the standard apply to library procedures and are suggested for other types of software, including utilities and application programs. Each programming language supplied by Digital and implemented on the VMS operating system lets users write programs to follow this standard.

The VAX/VMS Modular Programming Standard applies to procedures that have a public entry point, that is, one that the VMS Linker can locate by searching the default system libraries. This standard does not apply to calls of internal routines in procedures that do not have public entry points. This is true as long as the entire set of procedures follows the standard.

Coding Rules

The VAX/VMS Modular Programming Standard governs the following functions:

- The calling interface
- Initialization
- Reporting of exception conditions
- AST reentrance
- Resource allocation
- Format and content of coded modules

- Shareable images
- Upward compatibility

4.6.3 IEEE Standards

The Institute of Electrical and Electronics Engineers (IEEE) prepares standards for applying engineering principles to developing and maintaining software. Both new engineers and experienced engineers need to be aware of these standards. For new engineers, the standards serve as valuable guidelines to recommended practices. For experienced engineers, they serve as benchmarks against which to compare their own practices, particularly since the IEEE standards are the result of agreement among practicing professionals.

IEEE intends to review and update its standards every five years to ensure that they remain up-to-date. See Appendix C, Industry Standards, for a list of IEEE standards and source information for IEEE and other external standards.

4.7 Planning International Products

The international marketplace is growing rapidly. In international markets, the use of English and American standards and conventions are often unacceptable. An international software product has the following characteristics:

- It can be adapted to local needs by a group that is geographically remote from the product's developers.

- After any appropriate adaptation, it is equally attractive in all the markets.

The structure of the original product can make adaptation either simple or complex. Building a product that a local group can modify easily may require more time and care than building the product for one geographical market. However, Digital's development teams try to design products so that local engineering groups can adapt them easily. No definitive standards exist for designing international software products. However, Digital's experience in adapting software for use outside the United States has generated a number of guidelines that can improve the process.

For a discussion of these guidelines and the requirements of the international markets, see Appendix B, International Product Development.

In addition to designing the product for adaptation to international markets, development teams need to consider how to provide local engineering teams with the necessary project information to carry out their work. The local engineering team might need source code, kit-build procedures, the test system, specification documents, design documents, draft manuals, and so on. Project documents (product requirements, product specifications, and development plan) detail clearly the development team's plans to meet the needs of the local engineering groups. This information includes:

- Who the local engineering contacts are
- When the source code will be available
- How the source code will be delivered
- What engineering documents will be made available

Chapter 5

Design and Implementation

When preliminary planning and design are complete, the development team turns to the tasks of creating the detailed design, implementing it, and testing the software. The tasks entail building source code modules, then compiling, linking, and executing the resulting images. User documentation is created, and software tests are conducted to ensure that the implementation operates correctly.

Often, the system implementation consists of a series of stages or base levels in which each adds more and more of the required functionality. As the team implements and tests each base level, they may discover unforeseen problems in implementing the design, meaning that specifications and designs might require revision. If so, the programs, the tests, and the user documentation must also accurately reflect changes in requirements or designs.

The project team must analyze the structure and performance of the software in this phase. Reviews of the design, code, tests, and documentation are held frequently.

Other groups are given copies of the software to determine how well the program works under controlled conditions. Performance analysis ensures that the system will meet certain customer-environment requirements. When this phase is successfully completed, the project should have software that works.

Information about the design and implementation phase are covered in the following three chapters:

- This chapter, Chapter 5, discusses the major tasks of design and implementation:
  - Producing a detailed design
  - Writing design documents
  - Implementing base levels
  - Producing product kits
- Chapter 6, Coding Guidelines for Implementation, focuses on the coding conventions used for implementing the detailed design.
- Chapter 7, The Testing Process, concentrates on the testing process, which verifies the product against the design.

Figure 5–1 shows the relationships among the key engineering tasks and documents of design and implementation.

Figure 5–1: Design and Implementation Phase

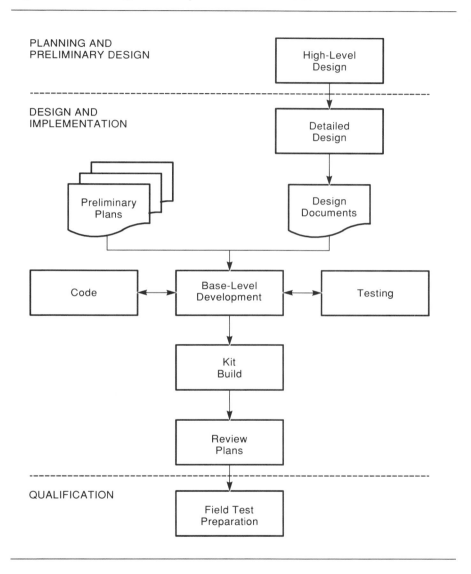

5.1 Detailed Design Process

Detailed design has two primary goals:

- To understand enough of the details of implementation to reduce the technical and schedule-related risks to an acceptable level
- To communicate and coordinate the activities associated with the implementation process

For several reasons, the development team usually does not complete all detailed designs before it starts coding:

- A detailed design that is not tightly coupled with the actual code is less likely to represent that code accurately as coding proceeds.
- Significant portions of the detailed designs are likely to change between early design work and coding. Such changes often occur when the product relies on external deliverables not yet fully specified.
- Additional design detail does not help developers to understand or reduce the risks.
- Extremely detailed design may best be expressed and communicated using a program design language. In the absence of such a language, the designers use the implementation language itself, blurring the line between design and coding.

At Digital, the development team determines both the form of the designs and the level of detail within them. The "acceptable level" of risk is usually reached by consensus among the team members. The team also decides how formal the process of communicating the detailed designs among the members will be.

The following list shows the main input-to and output-from the detailed design process.

- **Input**
  - Product requirements document
  - Alternatives/feasibility study
  - High-level design documents
  - Product specification

- **Output**
  - — Detailed design documents
  - — Functional prototype
  - — Performance/usability evaluation of prototype
  - — Implementation estimates
  - — Identification/evaluation of technical risks

5.1.1 Logical Modules and Physical Modules

As part of the detailed design process, the development team identifies the logical modules that are subsequently "packaged" into physical modules.

Logical modules represent the features and functions the application will have. Logical modules are packaged into physical modules that make up the application and accomplish the features delineated in the logical modules.

For example, a hypothetical application (SELF) is designed to be an online system that operates over Digital's DECnet network to provide "phone book" information about users on the network. SELF will have an online user interface program (UIP) and a data base server (DBS). The UIP will perform all of the user functions and reside on any of the nodes in the network that communicates with the data base server. Five physical modules will make up the UIP. One of these, UIPMAIN.BAS is the master module and incorporates six logical modules from the application's design:

- PROGRAM: UIP main program module
- LOCAL: Initialize UIP
- LOCAL: Terminate UIP
- LOCAL: Get a valid command
- LOCAL: Process a valid SELF command
- LOCAL: Error handling

Structure charts are useful for representing the relationships among logical and physical designs.

5.1.2 Design Documents

A design document is a set of files that represent the design of the product. These may take different forms:

- A written description of features of the code
- Pseudocode or high-level language code with embedded comments
- Data-flow diagrams, structure charts, and supplementary text

The main purpose of the detailed design document is to translate the high-level designs into module designs. These detailed designs sufficiently document designs and tests to permit coding of the software modules. In addition, the detailed designs, by relying on graphic representation, pseudocode, and written text, allow engineers with different programming language skills to participate in any design review. The detailed design process, including its review stages, helps to ensure that the product is taking shape properly and that component and system interfaces are adequately considered. Finally, the design documents serve as a resource for the maintenance team later in the product's life cycle.

5.2 Implementing Base Levels

A base level is the set of files and documents that make up a specific version of a product built at a specific time. It represents a particular level of features for the product. In effect, base levels are stages in the design, development, and maintenance of a product.

Base levels are important throughout the life cycle of the product. During implementation, they provide a way of measuring progress and a reference point for testing. During maintenance, they improve the chances that the maintenance team can recover and modify a previous version of the product.

5.2.1 Types of Base Levels

Projects have two types of base levels:

- Implementation base levels, which are used to develop and integrate levels of features for the product
- Maintenance base levels, which are used to correct problems or add minor enhancements to the product

Managing base levels is an ongoing job for the engineering project leader. The project leader assigns people to specific coding and testing activities. The project leader also tracks the team's progress relative to the development schedule. The project leader, and the development team, must also decide when to freeze the code, that is, when to stop changing a given set of modules for base-level testing.

5.2.2 Requirements Analysis

New requirements are an additional source of input for base-level development.

Although the development team tries to accurately gauge the requirements and market for the product, suggestions for the product may inspire changes throughout the development period. In conjunction with other members of the product team, the development team evaluates potential new requirements with respect to the following issues:

- What is the business need for this requirement?
- Is it possible to implement the requirement?
- If so, what is the impact on development and documentation, particularly on their schedules?
- What is the impact on training?
- Where does this requirement fit in a priority list?
- What does the product gain by adding this capability or feature?
- What does the product lose by not adding this capability or feature?
- Is it worth the cost (resources, impact on schedule) to implement it?
- Can this requirement be postponed until a subsequent release?

The team must understand the implications of implementing or not implementing a new requirement. The development team can indicate the cost of implementing a new requirement; product management indicates the benefits of fulfilling the new requirement.

If a suggestion is approved as a requirement for the current release, the team will need to update the project documents to reflect the addition. Base-level development will need to reflect the new task assignments. If the suggestion is not approved, the team may add it to the project's "wish list."

Sometimes, trade-offs must be made between market needs and time to market. In some cases, the team postpones fulfilling a particular requirement; in others, the demands of meeting the market needs win out, and the schedule is changed. All members of the product team must be aware of any decisions not to deliver some functional capability.

5.2.3 Build Procedures

Development teams at Digital plan their build procedures and describe them in the development plan. When possible, they use detailed command procedures from existing products to help automate the build process. They often use a combination of command procedures and the tools described in Chapter 2, Software Development Tools, such as the VAX DEC/Module Management System (DEC/MMS), VAX DEC/Test Manager, the VAX Language-Sensitive Editor (LSE), and the VAX DEC/Code Management System (DEC/CMS).

A number of problems can occur while the team is preparing base levels. Table 5–1 lists some of the more common problems and ways to deal with them.

Table 5–1: Problems in Preparing Base Levels

Problem	Response
Too many errors in new software during base-level build.	Halt the build process and assess the completeness of the new software. An additional review may be needed to confirm that the new software is ready for the base level.
Too many rebuilds of the software because it fails regression tests.	Make sure that all tests are run before rebuilding the system to minimize the number of builds needed for the system.
Failure of regression tests caused by coupling new software with old.	Make sure that any old test procedures that are replaced by new test procedures are marked as not applicable for the next base level. These may be applicable only for a specific base level and are not required for additional base-level tests.
Partially completed modules do not integrate properly in build.	Resist including partially completed modules in the base level. Either do not freeze and test the software during this base level or redefine the module so that it can be frozen in the base level.
Installation procedure and installation kits have errors.	To minimize the number of times the base-level build process is required, make sure that the distribution kits and installation procedures are tested thoroughly before the formal test period.

Teams at Digital use the following guidelines for the build procedure:

- Teams agree on general work procedures that allow members to manage development tasks efficiently and without conflicting with each other's work.

- After working on modules, team members run unit tests on the modules.

- After successful unit testing, team members link the modules and create the images for the full application.

- Team members then run functional and regression tests on the application. (See Section 7.3.2 for more information on regression testing.)

- Assuming the test and build cycle is successful, the modules are then checked back in to the DEC/CMS library. The team agrees upon and follows check-in procedures.
- Using DEC/MMS, DEC/Test Manager, and DEC/CMS, the team automates and tracks the steps of testing and building.

Once the modules reach an agreed-upon level of progress, the team creates a DEC/CMS class that represents the most recently attained base level and uses this class to produce software kits.

For more information on setting up build procedures and work procedures using the VAXset tools, see *A Methodology for Software Development Using VMS Tools*.

5.2.4 Product Kits

Development teams build kits at different points in the development of the product. In general, the team assembles kits only after completing a base level to ensure that the distributed software is stable. This approach also minimizes the effort needed to prepare the kits.

Product kits are needed for the following testing activities:

- Testing by the development group on separate systems with different versions of prerequisite software (for example, different versions of VMS)
- Testing by internal users
- Testing by external field test sites

The types of kits and the amount of testing associated with them vary. The product manager and development team determine the appropriate media types for the product. If the product's installation must be tested on all types of media, the team takes this into account as it considers kit building and plans for the field test process.

After all testing is complete and satisfactory, the final kit is submitted to manufacturing.

Chapter 6

Coding Guidelines for Implementation

During the design and implementation phase, the development team translates its designs into code. This chapter discusses general coding guidelines. Appendix A contains specific guidelines for coding in the C language.

The guidelines and coding conventions described in this chapter are applicable to a range of languages. It is important to adopt guidelines that promote consistent and efficient coding practices. This is particularly helpful to engineers unfamiliar with an application's code. It is also crucial for any future maintenance efforts on the software. Using a consistent coding style helps software engineers produce good programs. It allows engineers to adopt routines and data structures from existing software. This process is much easier if the existing software is readily understandable.

6.1 Selecting Guidelines

This section provides development teams with generic coding guidelines applicable to different languages. Guidelines provide consistency within a project and may ease the transition to another project. Language-specific guidelines for C are provided in Appendix A, Coding Conventions for VAX C.

6.1.1 Examine Existing Source Code

Because team members may work on a number of projects, it is important for them to adjust their styles to differences in conventions. It is usually appropriate to follow conventions established in any existing source code. In order to maintain an existing product, the source code should be consistent within an application. If it is necessary to use a different convention from the one already established in an application, the entire application is updated to reflect the new convention.

If modules from other projects are used, they are reformatted when practical to conform to the project's conventions. When a program contains undocumented code, comments are added to describe the code's function. These comments help simplify future software maintenance efforts.

6.1.2 Use the Language-Sensitive Editor

An excellent source of coding guidelines for new code is the VAX Language-Sensitive Editor (LSE). It provides one of the easiest ways for development teams to format code consistently. LSE has online language templates for these languages:

VAX Ada
VAX BASIC
VAX Bliss–32
VAX C
VAX CDD
VAX COBOL
VAX DATATRIEVE
VAX DIBOL
VAX DOCUMENT
VAX FORTRAN
VAX MACRO
VAX Pascal
VAX PL/I
VAX SCAN
VAXELN Pascal

The LSE language templates ensure consistent formatting, capitalization, indentation, and spacing. Although formatting standards are built into the templates, development teams can modify them for their own project and then save these modifications in an environment file. The environment file can then be stored in a central directory. When the team members log in to the system, they can automatically have access to the central directory via information stored in their login command file (LOGIN.COM). In this way, the modified templates can be shared by everyone who uses LSE.

In addition to providing formatting consistency, LSE provides much of the module and routine preface information for its supported languages.

6.1.3 Build Program Modules

A module is a single body of code and text that can be assembled and compiled as a unit. Generally, it is part of a larger program or facility created by linking all of the component modules and object code. A facility is a collection of one or more modules that implement a set of related functions or services.

A module has some self-evident identity. Typically, a module consists of either of the following:

- A single function or data base
- A collection of related functions, any one of which would be too small for an independent module

The module's interface should be as clean as possible. Try to avoid side effects. When they occur, document them in the routine header.

The goal in module design is to maximize cohesion and minimize coupling. Cohesion is the degree to which the tasks performed by a single program module are functionally related. Coupling is a measure of the interdependence among modules.

The following sections describe the elements typically included in a module at Digital. The inclusion of these elements is simplified by the use of LSE and its standard module templates for all coding activities. On the following pages, Bliss templates are used as examples.

To access the standard LSE module template for any VAX language, the developer must first use LSE to create a file of the appropriate language type. For example, to create the Bliss source file named EXAMPLE that appears below, the developer first invokes LSE by entering a VMS command and specifying the name of the file to be created as EXAMPLE.BLI (BLI is the three-letter VMS file type used to identify Bliss source files). In response, LSE opens the file and associates it with the standard LSE Bliss template.

The template and file are linked by the single string *[~MODULE~]*, which LSE writes into the file as it creates it. Known as a *placeholder*, this special keyword allows the developer to either call up the complete Bliss module template through LSE keyboard commands or to bypass it by deleting or typing over the placeholder.

Example 6–1 reproduces the standard LSE Bliss module template that appears when the placeholder *[~MODULE~]* is expanded. This expanded template contains placeholders of its own for such elements as the title and module level declarations. These in turn can be expanded, deleted, or typed over and are discussed below.

6.1.3.1 Module Preface

At Digital, a module opens with a preface that documents its function, use, and history. As shown in Example 6–1, developers at Digital include the following elements:

❶ Title statement

The title statement specifies the title line in the listing file.

❷ Module statement

The module statement specifies the module name. If the object file is inserted into an object library, this module name that appears in a listing of the object library's contents. This name also appears in a LINK map.

❸ Copyright statement

Example 6–1: LSE Template for a Bliss Module Preface

```
[~%TITLE '[~quoted_chars~]'~]                    ❶
MODULE {~name~} [~(module_switches)~] =          ❷
BEGIN
!
! COPYRIGHT (c) 1988 BY                           ❸
! COMPANY XYZ, ANYWHERE, USA.
! ALL RIGHTS RESERVED.
!
! THIS SOFTWARE IS FURNISHED UNDER A LICENSE AND MAY BE USED AND COPIED
! ONLY  IN  ACCORDANCE  OF  THE  TERMS  OF  SUCH  LICENSE  AND WITH THE
! INCLUSION OF THE ABOVE COPYRIGHT NOTICE. THIS SOFTWARE OR  ANY  OTHER
! COPIES THEREOF MAY NOT BE PROVIDED OR OTHERWISE MADE AVAILABLE TO ANY
! OTHER PERSON.  NO TITLE TO AND  OWNERSHIP OF THE  SOFTWARE IS  HEREBY
! TRANSFERRED.
!
! THE INFORMATION IN THIS SOFTWARE IS  SUBJECT TO CHANGE WITHOUT NOTICE
! AND  SHOULD  NOT  BE  CONSTRUED  AS A COMMITMENT BY COMPANY XYZ.
!
! COMPANY XYX ASSUMES NO RESPONSIBILITY FOR THE USE  OR  RELIABILITY OF
! ITS SOFTWARE ON EQUIPMENT WHICH IS NOT SUPPLIED BY COMPANY XYZ.
!++
! FACILITY:                                       ❹
!
!    [~tbs~]
!
! ABSTRACT:                                       ❺
!
!    [~tbs~]
!
! AUTHORS:                                        ❻
!
!    [~tbs~]
!
! CREATION DATE: [~tbs~]                          ❼
!
! MODIFICATION HISTORY:                           ❽
!--
[~module_level_declarations~]                     ❾
[~routine_declaration~]...                        ❿
END                           ! End of module
ELUDOM
```

A standard copyright statement appears on the first page of every source file. Note the following about the copyright statement:

— When developing a new module, the year stated is the year of the first release, not the year coding begins.

— When modifying an existing program that has legal notices, verify the validity of the statements. Add the year that the code is changed to the existing copyright year. Separate the years with a comma.

❹ Facility statement

A module may be a dedicated part of a larger linked facility, part of several facilities, or a general-purpose library function. The facility statement identifies the whole of which the module is part.

❺ Abstract

The abstract briefly describes the function of the module, including the design basis for any critical algorithms. If the module needs an extensive functional description, it appears on the next page.

❻ Authors

❼ Creation date

❽ Modification history

The modification history provides the detailed history of changes made to the module, including the versions, the person editing the module, and the last date of each version. It also lists the specific changes made between base levels (during production) or releases, along with a short description of each problem and its solution, and appropriate references to related information.

Each history entry receives a maintenance number starting with 1. The maintenance numbers increase by one, are decimal, and are never reset. Generally, the entries are ordered starting with the most recent modification first; however, inherited code may preclude this type of ordering. The goal is to maintain the chronological consistency of entries among application modules. Engineers can also use the maintenance numbers to attach maintenance comments to all the lines of source code that were modified.

Note, however, that Digital's DEC/Code Management System (DEC/CMS) can generate much of this change history automatically. If the history attribute is defined for an element (typically an application module), DEC/CMS includes the element history in the output file when an engineer retrieves it from the DEC/CMS library. The element history is a list of the transactions that created each generation of the element. Each transaction record consists of the generation number, user, date, time, and remark associated with the command. The history attribute is defined by using the /HISTORY qualifier with either the CREATE ELEMENT or the MODIFY ELEMENT command.

If the notes and position attributes are both defined, DEC/CMS embeds notes in the output file when the element is retrieved. Notes are generation numbers embedded in the lines of the file. They indicate the generation in which the line was inserted or modified most recently. Notes appear at the horizontal position in the line specified by the position attribute. Engineers can obtain the same type of generation information by using the ANNOTATE command. Annotated listings include a replacement history and generation numbers that indicate when each line was inserted or modified most recently.

⑨ Module level declarations

When expanded, this placeholder provides a template for the module's declarations.

⑩ Routine declaration

When expanded, this placeholder provides a menu of routines.

6.1.3.2 Module Declarations

Example 6–2 shows what happens when you expand the MODULE_ LEVEL_DECLARATIONS placeholder of Example 6–1.

The format is that of a Bliss template, but is used for other languages. It contains the following sections:

❶ Table of contents

For Bliss, this lists, in order, all forward routine declarations with a summary description of each.

❷ Include files

Lists the specification of INCLUDE files or binary definitions. Lists library REQUIRE FILES and library macros that define MACROs, assembly parameters, systemwide equated symbols, and table definitions.

Example 6–2: LSE Template for a Bliss Module's Declaration

```
        .
        .
        .
! MODIFICATION HISTORY:
!--
!
!
! TABLE OF CONTENTS:               ❶
!
[~forward_routine_declaration~]
!
! INCLUDE FILES:                   ❷
!
[~library_declaration~]...
[~require_declaration~]...
!
! MACROS:                          ❸
!
[~macro_or_keywordmacro_declaration~]...
!
! EQUATED SYMBOLS:                 ❹
!
[~literal_declaration~]
[~bind_declaration~]
!
! OWN STORAGE:                     ❺
!
[~own_declaration~]
[~global_declaration~]
!
! EXTERNAL REFERENCES:             ❻
!
[~external_declarations~]...
[~routine_declaration~]...
END                                ! End of module
ELUDOM
```

❸ Macros

Defines local macros other than structure definitions.

❹ Equated symbols

Lists LITERAL and BIND declarations.

❺ Own storage

Lists declaration of permanent storage allocations and local storage structures.

❻ External references

List the specification of externals. For assembly language, only WEAK or VALIDATION externals need to be listed.

6.1.3.3 Procedure Description

If you now expand the ROUTINE_DECLARATION placeholder in Example 6–1 and choose the complex routine option from an LSE-generated menu, you get template additions shown in Example 6–3. (Note that in Example 6–3, the MODULE_LEVEL_DECLARATIONS placeholder is not expanded, nor is there a copyright statement.)

Example 6–3:   LSE Template for a Bliss Routine

```
          .
          .
          .
[~%TITLE '[~quoted_chars~]'~]
MODULE {~name~} [~(module_switches)~] =
BEGIN
!++
! FACILITY:
!
!    [~tbs~]
!
! ABSTRACT:
!
!    [~tbs~]
!
! AUTHORS:
!
!    [~tbs~]
!
! CREATION DATE: [~tbs~]
!
! MODIFICATION HISTORY:
!--
```

Example 6–3 Cont'd. on next page

Example 6–3 (Cont.): LSE Template for a Bliss Routine

```
[~module_level_declarations~]
!
[~%SBTTL '[~quoted_chars~]'~]
[~GLOBAL~] ROUTINE {~name~}[~(formals)~] : [~routine_attributes~]... =
!++
! FUNCTIONAL DESCRIPTION:                              ❶
!
!    [~tbs~]
!
! FORMAL PARAMETERS:                                   ❷
!
!    [~description_or_none~]
!
! IMPLICIT INPUTS:                                     ❸
!
!    [~description_or_none~]
!
! IMPLICIT OUTPUTS:                                    ❹
!
!    [~description_or_none~]
!
! {~routine_value_or_completion_codes~}               ❺
!
!    [~description_or_none~]
!
! SIDE EFFECTS:                                        ❻
!
!    [~description_or_none~]
!--
    BEGIN
    [~declaration~]...
    {~expression~}...
    END;
[~routine_declaration~]...
END                                  ! End of module
ELUDOM
```

Include the elements of a procedure description shown in Example 6–3 whether they are actually present or not.

❶ Functional description

This section describes a procedure's purpose and documents its interfaces. The description includes the rationale for using any critical algorithms, including literature references, where applicable. Indicate in this section the reentrance characteristics of this procedure if they differ from those given in the module's description.

❷ Formal parameters

Parameters conform to the VAX Procedure Calling and Condition Handling Standard. For routines that conform to the calling standard, the argument list pointer AP always points to the base of the caller-supplied argument list. Bliss and MACRO routines local to a module can pass arguments in registers.

The description of the arguments also includes the following:

- How the arguments are passed:
  - By value
  - By reference
  - By descriptor
- Type of parameter (for untyped languages such as Bliss)
- Mode of the parameter:
  - Read-only
  - Write-only
  - Read-write

❸ Implicit inputs

List any inputs from storage, internal or external to the module, that are not specified in the argument list. Usually all that will appear here is NONE.

❹ Implicit outputs

List any outputs to internal or external storage that are not specified in the argument list.

❺ Completion status or routine value

List the success or failure condition value symbols that could be returned as completion codes in R0. If a procedure returns a function value other than a condition value in R0, change the heading to routine value.

❻ Side effects

In this section, describe any functional side effects not evident from a procedure's calling sequence. Such side effects include changes in storage allocation, process status, file operations, and possible signaled conditions. In general, document anything out of the ordinary that the procedure does to the environment. If a side effect modifies local or global storage locations, document this modification in the implicit output description.

Example 6–4 shows an expanded LSE template for a C module. Note the similarity between the C module preface and that for Bliss shown in Example 6–3.

Example 6–4:   LSE Template for a C Module

```
[@#module@]
/*
**++
**   FACILITY:
**
**      [@tbs@]
**
**   ABSTRACT:
**
**      [@tbs@]
**
**   AUTHORS:
**
**      [@tbs@]
**
**
**   CREATION DATE:     [@tbs@]
**
**   MODIFICATION HISTORY:
**--
**/
[@include_files@]
[@macro_definitions@]

[@preprocessor_line@]...

[@comment@]...
```

Example 6–4 Cont'd. on next page

Example 6–4 (Cont.):   LSE Template for a C Module

```
/*
**++
**   FUNCTIONAL DESCRIPTION:
**
**       [@tbs@]
**
**   FORMAL PARAMETERS:
**
**       [@description_or_none@]
**
**   IMPLICIT INPUTS:
**
**       [@description_or_none@]
**
**   IMPLICIT OUTPUTS:
**
**       [@description_or_none@]
**
**   {@function_value_or_completion_codes@}
**
**       [@description_or_none@]
**
**   SIDE EFFECTS:
**
**       [@description_or_none@]
**
**--
**/
{@main() OR main function that accept arguments from the command line@}
{
    [@block_decl@]...

    {@statement@}...
}
[@function_definition@]...
```

Note that the called procedure specifies how it is to be called. The calling procedure must invoke the procedure correctly. The procedure description provides all the necessary information to determine how a routine is to be called.

6.1.3.4 Examples of LSE Language Constructs

The previous examples show how LSE provides the text elements for the module and routine prefaces. LSE also provides language construct templates for all its supported languages.

For example, working with the routine declaration section of the Bliss template brings you to the EXPRESSION placeholder. When expanded, it displays a menu of expressions from which to choose. The IF expression produces the following template:

```
IF {~expression~}
THEN
    {~expression~}
[~ELSE   {~expression~} ~];
[~expression~]...
END;
```

You could quickly fill in the EXPRESSION placeholder information by typing over the new placeholders:

```
IF test
THEN
    consequence
ELSE
    alternative;
[~expression~]...
END;
```

The following example shows an LSE template for a WHILE statement in C.

```
while ({@expression@})
    {@statement@}
[@statement@]...
```

Directly typing over the placeholders produces the following generic WHILE statement:

```
while (test)
    loop-body;
[@statement@]...
```

The templates represent accepted standards for effective language formatting, complete with indenting, capitalization, and spacing. A team can choose to modify the templates, in effect creating new conventions for the project. The key point is that formatting conventions are readily available and, through the use of LSE, can be applied consistently to code.

6.2 Choosing an Implementation Language

Because the software being developed today is increasingly complex and diverse, development teams need to carefully assess their choice of implementation language. Increasingly, development teams at Digital take advantage of the strengths and features of particular languages, based on the needs of the application being developed.

The key elements to consider when choosing an implementation language are as follows:

- The development team will use a non-machine-dependent, high-level language.
- Project plans will indicate the implementation language chosen and the rationale for the choice.

For the most part, the languages supported by Digital have equivalent features. All conform to the VAX Procedure Calling and Conditioning Standard and can be used in a multilanguage environment. They are supported by Digital tools such as LSE, VAX Source Code Analyzer (VAX SCA), and the VMS Debugger. Most have comparable compile times and execution times. However, these are not the most important issues when choosing an implementation language. Rather, consider the following issues:

- Will this software ever need to be ported to another operating system?
- Will this software ever need to be ported to another hardware target?
- What languages do the engineers on the project already know? How hard will it be to hire or train new people?
- How much code does the product have? How much will it share?
- What special language features does the application need? Does the language being considered provide them?
- Will the team be doing low-level or high-level programming? Does the language readily allow for this?

Each language has merits that can justify its use. For example, C is a viable choice for those products to be offered on multiple operating systems or multiple hardware targets. It is a good choice for products to be transported to and from comparable C environments and for applications that run with DECwindows.

Ada, a high-level language developed to highlight any portability problems, is suitable for those projects that need to develop products only for VMS. Besides providing powerful language features, Ada reduces software life cycle costs by providing for modularization and separate compilation using packages, scope rules, and a compilation data base. Ada also allows both bottom-up and top-down program development, while enhancing software reliability through strong typing.

6.3 Improving Code Readability

Other readers can better understand source code if it is properly structured, organized, and indented. The code should be constructed into blocks with a limited amount of branching. In general, low-level constructs should be indented more than high-level constructs. This approach provides a visual indication of the control flow and allows other engineers to better understand and modify it.

Regardless of the source of a project's coding guidelines, the conventions described in the following sections have been shown to improve the readability of programs:

- Symbols
- Case conventions
- Spacing conventions
- Formatting comments

6.3.1 Symbols

To ensure code readability it is best to use symbols, not numbers, as much as possible. Because symbols are mnemonic, they clarify programs and provide more information for cross-reference listings. It is good coding practice to define a symbol for a constant that is used a number of times. If the value for that symbol changes, the symbol's value will need to redefined only once rather than in every place it is used in the program. Thus, using symbols simplifies the task of maintenance and facilitates cross-referencing.

6.3.2 Case Conventions

Case conventions should be appropriate to the language. Using all uppercase letters for the code is not desirable because it is difficult to read. Avoid randomly scattering uppercase and lowercase letters in the code. In general, keywords are one case, identifiers another. For example, in Ada, where formatting conventions are more stringent, you are expected to use lowercase letters for keywords and uppercase letters for identifiers.

The C language distinguishes between uppercase and lowercase letters in variable names and keywords. To ensure portability, global symbols must never require case distinction. Lowercase letters are appropriate for variable and function names, structure names, and keywords. Use uppercase letters for preprocessor identifiers (macro names), symbols defined with the VAX extension facilities *globalref*, *globaldef*, and *globalvalue* to ensure correct access. Finally, if a symbol is created that is external and has mixed case, all references to it must match the case of the definition and the name must not conflict with other symbols that have the same characters but different case.

Use uppercase and lowercase letters for all comments. Comments that are complete sentences start with a capital letter and end with a period.

When using languages that do not distinguish between uppercase and lowercase letters, your development team should not depend heavily on using case conventions as a way to convey vital information about the code because they may be difficult to thoroughly enforce.

Example 6–5 shows how to use uppercase and lowercase letters properly in a Pascal program.

Example 6–5: Proper Capitalization in a Pascal Program

```
{ Program to call LIB_LP_LINES and determine the
{ number of lines per line printer page.
}
PROGRAM lines (OUTPUT);

{ Declare the external procedure used by this
{ program.
}
FUNCTION lib_lp_lines : INTEGER; EXTERN;

{ Call lib_lp_lines and print the result.
}
BEGIN
    WRITELN('Each page contains ',lib_lp_lines,' lines.');
END.
```

6.3.3 Spacing

Digital developers use the following spacing guidelines when permitted by the coding language.

- Follow a comma (,) with a single space.

- Follow and precede an equal sign (=) with a single space.

- Follow an exclamation mark (!) or semicolon (;) with a single space, to separate a comment from the source code.

- Precede and follow the arithmetic operators plus (+) and minus (−) by spaces in expressions.

- Use blank lines to separate logically distinct (but physically close) pieces of code.

- Be aware that appropriate spacing in code often makes it easier to read.

- Use form feeds between routines.

The BASIC program in Example 6–6 shows proper spacing in a BASIC program.

Example 6–6: Spacing in a BASIC Program

```
10      ! The following BASIC program converts a character
        ! string representing a hexadecimal value to a
        ! longword, then adds one to the result.

        ! Declare the external routine used.
        !
        EXTERNAL LONG FUNCTION OTS_CVT_TZ_L

        ! Perform the conversion.
        !
        HEXVAL_ = "80012BFA"
        RET_STAT% = OTS_CVT_TZ_L (HEXVAL_, HEX%)

        ! Add one to the result.
        !
        HEX% = HEX% + 1

        END
```

6.3.4 Formatting Comments

The importance of including comments cannot be overemphasized. In any professional environment, many people will read the code. Sometimes they will want to modify it to do something else; at other times they will want to modify it to do what was originally intended.

A comment describes the purpose of a section of code. If written properly, the code itself conveys this adequately. Most comments describe what a source statement does. This category of comment is imperative in form, as shown in the examples in this section.

This section describes how to format block comments and line comments, and how to use LSE to format comments.

6.3.4.1 Block Comments

Digital developers comment on blocks of statements by writing one or more lines of text preceding the block. Comment lines begin with comment delimiters appropriate to the particular language. Example 6–7 shows an example of a FORTRAN program with exclamation points being used as a delimiter. Frequently, the last comment line contains only the comment delimiter. You may wish to set off block comments with blank lines to make them easier to read. Comment delimiters are followed by one space, as shown in Example 6–7.

Example 6–7: Block Comments in a FORTRAN Program

```
! This program demonstrates a call to the
! Run-Time Library procedure STR_PREFIX.

! Initialize the strings to be used.
!
AS = "ABC"
BS = "DEF"

! Call STR_PREFIX
!
ISTAT = STR_PREFIX (AS, BS)

END
```

When possible, indent the comment delimiter the same as the source code it discusses, with the comment text separated by a single space. Note that LSE automatically indents the delimiter this way. Never write a comment that could be interpreted as a language statement. Always include a block comment at the beginning of a major segment of the program.

6.3.4.2 Line Comments

You can write brief comments on the same line as the statements they describe. Be sure to indent them enough to separate them from the statements. If more than one line comment appears in a block of code, each new comment starts at the same position, as shown in Example 6–8.

Example 6–8: Justified Line Comments in a C Program

```
while ( !finish()) {          /* Main sequence:*/
    inquire ();               /* Get user request*/
    process ();               /* And carry it out*/
}                             /* As long as possible*/
```

Note that all line comments start at some specific column and are flagged by a slash and an asterisk (/*). Compare Example 6–9 to Example 6–8.

Example 6–9: Unjustified Line Comments in a C Program

```
while (!finish()) { /* Main sequence: */
    inquire(); /* Get user request */
    process(); /* And carry it out */
} /* As long as possible */
```

In general, it is best to use line comments to document variable definitions and block comments to describe the computation process. Example 6–8 would best be written as a block comment, as shown in Example 6–10.

Example 6–10: Block Comment in a C Program

```
/*
 * Main sequence: get and process all user requests.
 */
while ( !finish()) {
    inquire ();
    process ();
}
```

6.3.4.3 Formatting Comments with LSE

Because LSE recognizes many of the comment portions of the code, you can use LSE to format them. In addition, LSE treats comments specially when a placeholder is erased or duplicated. Two commands are useful: ALIGN and FILL.

When you use the ALIGN command, LSE lines up all the comments within a region along the same columns. For example, here is a commented program section:

```
IF (col >= R_Margin)   ! This is the start of an
THEN                   ! extended end-of-line comment block
   Begin
    i := i + 1 ;
    j := j + i ;  ! another comment
  ! to be filled
```

After you use the ALIGN command, the program section looks like this:

```
IF (col >= R_Margin)       ! This is the start of an
THEN                       ! extended end-of-line comment block
   Begin
    i := i + 1 ;
    j := j + i ;           ! another comment
                           ! to be filled
```

When you use the FILL command, LSE aligns and fills out each comment line. For example, here is the same program section after using the FILL command:

```
IF (col >= R_Margin)       ! This is the start of an extended
THEN                       ! end-of-line comment block
   Begin
    i := i + 1 ;
    j := j + i ;           ! another comment to be filled
```

Special handling of comments applies only to a trailing comment; that is, one that is the last item on a line, excluding blank space. LSE recognizes two types of comments: bracketed comments and line comments. A bracketed comment has both a beginning and ending delimiter; a line comment begins with a delimiter but terminates with the end of the line.

6.4 Naming Conventions

Naming conventions are used in naming files, directories, facilities, modules, procedures, program sections (PSECTs), and variables. The naming conventions discussed in this section make it easier for development teams to carry out their work. They also make it easier for maintenance teams to carry out theirs. See the *Guide to Creating VMS Modular Procedures* for additional naming conventions.

NOTE

This section discusses software structures such as file names, directories, and procedures. Any such structures supplied by Digital have a dollar sign ($) in their name. The use of the dollar sign ($) in the names of these software structures is reserved for Digital.

To eliminate any possible conflict resulting from duplicate names, do not use dollar signs ($) in the names of any software structures you create. Instead, use an underscore (_) character.

6.4.1 File Names

The purpose of a file-naming convention is to make the file names of a product family or facility more consistent, organized, and easier to identify. When you use such a convention, it will be easier to identify which files are part of a particular software product family.

All file names use the following format:

```
fac_<IDENTIFIER>_<PURPOSE>.<FILE_TYPE>
```

The different parts of the syntax have the following meanings:

fac_	The product's unique facility name, followed by an underscore (_) character
<IDENTIFIER>	An identifier string (optional)
_	Underscore character to separate parts
<PURPOSE>	A string that identifies the purpose of the file
<FILE_TYPE>	A string that identifies the type of data the file contains

The facility name (fac) is a unique alphanumeric string containing from 2 to 27 characters (2 to 4 characters are suggested). This string is used as a prefix to uniquely identify a product and its components, including file names. Facility names you supply should be followed by an underscore (_) to identify the software not supplied by Digital.

The optional identifier string (IDENTIFIER) makes it possible to have multiple files that serve the same purpose. Products that have multiple files serving a similar purpose (for instance, more than one shareable image library file, help file, startup file, and so on) need to include the identifier string. Products that do not have multiple files serving a similar purpose do not need to include the identifier string.

For example, if a product named Employee List has one startup file, no identifier string is needed:

`EMPLOYEES_STARTUP.COM`

A file type string (FILE TYPE) is a character string from 1 to 39 characters (3 or 4 characters are suggested) that identifies the file based on its contents. When choosing a file type, consider a default file type before creating a new one. Using a default file type helps to limit the number of unique file types that reside on the system.

Software products often use files that are common to many products. Some examples of commonly used files are help files, message files, and run-time libraries. If your goal is to make the names of these files more consistent, all products using these types of files should comply with this standard.

Table 6–1 lists the common files and their associated naming convention.

Table 6–1: Naming Conventions for Common Files

Type of File	Naming Convention
Help files	fac_<IDENTIFIER>_HELP.HLB
Main images	fac_<IDENTIFIER>_MAIN.EXE
Message files	fac_<IDENTIFIER>_MSG.EXE
RTL images	fac_<IDENTIFIER>_RTL.EXE
Shareable images	fac_<IDENTIFIER>_SHR.EXE
Object libraries	fac_<IDENTIFIER>_OBJLIB.OLB
Option files	fac_<IDENTIFIER>_OPTION.OPT
Startup files	fac_<IDENTIFIER>_STARTUP.COM
Release notes	fac_<version>.RELEASE_NOTES
Control programs	fac_<IDENTIFIER>_CONTROL.EXE
Initialization files	fac_<IDENTIFIER>_INIT.INI
G Float RTL Images	fac_<IDENTIFIER>_RTL_G.EXE
H Float RTL Images	fac_<IDENTIFIER>_RTL_H.EXE
Client images	fac_CLIENT_<purpose>
Server images	fac_SERVER_<purpose>

The following examples show how to name client and server files properly for the hypothetical product VAX QUALITY. The file type .COM stands for a command file, and the file type .EXE stands for an executable file.

```
QUAL_CLIENT_MAIN.EXE

QUAL_SERVER_MAIN.EXE

QUAL_CLIENT_STARTUP.COM

QUAL_SERVER_STARTUP.COM

QUAL_CLIENT_SHR.EXE

QUAL_SERVER_SHR.EXE

QUAL_CLIENT_MSG.EXE

QUAL_SERVER_OPTIONS.OPT
```

```
QUAL_RTL.EXE

QUAL_OBJLIB.OLB

QUAL_HELP.HLB

QUAL_INIT.INI

QUAL_010.RELEASE_NOTES
```

6.4.2 Directories

Top-level directory names must be consistent with the file-naming convention. Correct directory names contain the following:

- The product's unique facility name
- The underscore (_) character
- An identifier string

The following example shows a top-level directory name for a product called Employees List:

```
EMPLOYEES_SERVER.DIR
```

6.4.3 Procedures

When you create a procedure and give it a global name, other procedures in the same image can call it. In such an environment, global procedures require a naming convention to prevent any name conflict between global procedures in the same image.

The rules for naming entry points to procedures have this general form:

```
fac_<SYMBOL>
```

fac	A 2- to 4-character facility name, followed by an underscore (_) character.
<SYMBOL>	A symbol from 1 to 27 characters long. (The entire procedure name may not exceed 31 characters in length.)

The procedure name usually consists of a verb and its object, which describe the action of the procedure. For example, a run-time library procedure that calls a procedure STR_PREFIX might be called called LIB_GET_STR.

Some procedures, even though assigned global names, are not intended to be called from outside the facility in which they are located. These procedures are only available internally, within a set of procedures, and do not by themselves provide any features for the facility. The names of these procedures you supply contain three underscores (_ _ _). (Three underscores are necessary to avoid conflict condition value symbols you define that use two underscores.)

The names in Table 6–2 are examples of procedure entry point names.

Table 6–2: Examples of Entry Point Names

Procedure Name	Description
LIB_PRINT_REPORT	Global procedures supplied by you
LIB_ _ _ ADD_TAX	Internal procedure supplied by you

6.4.4 Modules

Module names are identical to file names except that module names do not include file types.

Table 6–3 contains examples of module names with corresponding file and procedure names.

Table 6–3: Relationships Among File, Module, and Procedure Names

File Name	Module Name	Procedure Name
LIB_SPR.B32	LIB_SPR	LIB_GET_SPR
		LIB_FREE_SPR
MTH_EXP.MAR	MTH_EXP	MTH_EXP

6.4.5 Variables

This section describes naming conventions for local and global variables.

6.4.5.1 Global Variables

Use the following format to name global variables:

```
fac_Gt_variablename
```

The letter G indicates this is a global variable; the letter t indicates the contents and use of the global variable. Table 6–4 lists the possible values for t.

Table 6–4: Global Variable Code Values

Value for t	Content and Use
A	Address
B	Byte integer
C	Single character
D	D_floating
E	Reserved for Digital
F	F_floating
G	G_floating
H	H_floating
I	Reserved for integer extensions
J	Reserved for customers for escape to other codes
K	Constant
L	Longword integer
M	Field mask
N	Numeric string (all byte forms)
O	Octaword
P	Packed string

Table 6–4 (Cont.):   Global Variable Code Values

Value for t	Content and Use
Q	Quadword integer
R	Records (structure)
S	Field size
T	Text (character) string
U	Smallest unit of addressable storage
V	Bit field
W	Word integer
X	Context dependent (generic)
Y	Context dependent (generic)
Z	Unspecified or nonstandard

The format for addressable global arrays is similar:

```
fac_At_variablename
```

The letter *A* represents a global array; the letter *t* corresponds to the values in Table 6–4.

6.4.5.2   Local Variables

Local values follow the same format as global variables, except that they lack the letter *G*, which indicates that a variable is global.

Use the following format to name local variables:

```
fac_t_variablename
```

The letter *t* indicates the contents and use of the variable. Table 6–4 lists the possible values for *t*.

6.4.6 Naming Conventions for Objects

Table 6–5 contains naming conventions for common objects.

Table 6–5: Naming Conventions for Objects

Object	Syntax
Facility-specific public macro names	_fac_ _<MACRONAME>
System macros using local symbols or macros	_fac_<MACRONAME>
System lock identifiers	fac_<FACILITY><SYSTEMLOCK>
PSECT names	fac_<PSECT_NAME>
Status code and condition values	fac_ _<STATUS>
Data structure definitions	fac_K_CLASS_<SYMBOLIC_CODE>[1]or fac_ K_DTYPE_<SYMBOLIC_CODE>
Rights data base identifiers	fac_<RIGHTS_IDENTIFIER>
Queue names	fac_<QUEUE_NAME>

[1]The different symbolic codes are listed in *Introduction to VMS System Routines*.

6.4.7 File Image IDs

The guidelines in this section apply to using the file image ID field in .EXE files. You can see these fields by issuing an ANALYZE/IMAGE command on any .EXE files. Any .EXE file belonging to a layered product should conform to these standards.

6.4.7.1 Image File ID and Image Name Fields

VMS layered products use the image file ID field to identify the product name and version number.

The field is 15 characters long and has the following format:

```
<PRODUCT NAME> <VERSION IDENTIFIER>
```

The VMS Linker option IDENT = "15-byte string" sets this field. In this case, the quotation marks must be used to delimit the string.

The image file ID field specifies the product name and version number; therefore, the image name of the file is acceptable in this field. Because VMS puts the image name in this field by default, you do not need to do so.

6.4.7.2 Shareable Images

Some products use images that are shareable or that another group in your organization supplies. In these cases, the group that provides the image sets the image file ID area to reflect the current version of the shareable image. The image ID then contains the information of the base product to which it belongs.

For example, if you used an image (NLQ_SHR.EXE), the image ID area of that executable image would be similar to the following:

```
IMAGE FILE ID:    NLQ V3.5-2
IMAGE NAME:       NLQ_SHR
```

6.5 Code Reviews

The project's development plan describes code review requirements. The purpose of code reviews is essentially the same as for design reviews or requirements reviews: to enhance the quality of the product. To this end, code reviews supplement the testing process described in Chapter 7. The reviews can be less formal—walkthroughs—or can entail formal inspection procedures.

6.5.1 Informal Walkthroughs

The code walkthrough process is similar to that for design reviews (see Section 4.5). Typically informal, code walkthroughs can take place during group meetings. The team holds walkthroughs as soon as possible after engineers write the code and complete unit testing.

During code walkthroughs, the development team tries to accomplish the following:

- Find errors in the code
- Make sure code comments are complete and accurate
- Ensure coding standards are followed
- Show new engineers on the team what is expected of their code, particularly any group-specific methodology
- Help engineers become familiar with code other than their own
- Provide a forum for experienced engineers to share their knowledge with less experienced engineers

6.5.2 Formal Inspections

Formal inspections are a type of technical peer review in which a small group of engineers, led by a trained moderator, examines a process document line-by-line to find problems. This process can be used for any type of review.

At Digital, the engineer's supervisor selects and assigns the inspectors. Each inspector contributes unique technical expertise to the inspection. The supervisor does not attend the inspection. Typically four to six people attend a single inspection, which lasts about 2 hours. The reviewers are able to inspect about 500 lines of text or 250 lines of code (excluding comments).

In every inspection, the document under review is compared with one or more source documents. For example, module code may have pseudocode as a source document along with the product specification and design documents as supporting documents. As the inspectors discover problems, they record and classify them by problem type. When the inspection is complete, the engineer receives a list of the problems found and their classification. The engineer is responsible for correcting the problems.

The factor that limits formal inspections is the availability of time and personnel. The time necessary for formal inspections must be built in to what is often a tight schedule. The key to planning inspections is to identify those documents that are to be inspected because of their audience or importance.

Most inspections uncover at least one problem that could otherwise result in a problem report. The cost of a formal inspection can be justified because it requires only about half the time needed for dealing with a problem report. Managers should encourage scheduling the time needed for formal inspections; otherwise development teams may forego them. In spite of these constraints, formal inspections remain one option for helping ensure improved product quality.

6.5.3 Code Inspection Guidelines

At Digital the following questions are a part of any code inspection:

Function

1. Is there a concept, an underlying idea, that can be expressed easily in plain language? Is it expressed in plain language in the implemented code?
2. Does the function of this part have a clear place in the function of the whole? Is this function clearly expressed?
3. Is the routine properly sheltered so that it can perform its function reliably in spite of possible misuse?

Form

1. Is the style clean and clear?
2. Is it meaningful to all classes of readers who will see it?
3. Are there repeated code segments, whether within or between routines?
4. Are comments useful or are they an excuse for poor coding?
5. Is the level of detail consistent?
6. Are standard practices followed?
7. Is initialization done properly and does the routine clean up after initialization?

Economy

1. Are there redundant operations for which there is no compensating benefit?
2. Is storage use consistent both internally and with external specifications?
3. How much will it cost to modify? (Consider the three most likely modifications.)
4. Is it simple?

Chapter 7

The Testing Process

After a program has been coded, it is tested. The testing process is a part of the design and implementation phase. The primary goal of testing is to make sure that the application performs as described in the requirements and specifications documents. The benefit of testing is that it reduces the long-term costs of the application by finding and fixing code errors early in the development process when they are relatively cheap to correct. The software maintenance costs are similarly reduced.

As a part of the testing process, the development team considers the following:

- Levels of testing
- Types of tests
- Regression testing
- Testing and design
- Performance testing

Another type of testing, field testing, is discussed in Chapter 8, Qualification.

Throughout this chapter, frequent reference is made to the following Digital products, which are useful in the testing process:

- VAX DEC/Code Management System (DEC/CMS)
- VAX Performance and Coverage Analyzer (VAX PCA)
- VAX DEC/Test Manager

Figure 7–1 shows where testing fits in the development process. The product develops in a series of progressive base levels, each marking a new or different level of product features. Testing is required at each stage of development. Two levels of testing are done: unit testing and integrated testing. Regression testing is used to evaluate the results. These tests, which are described in the following sections, form part of the full application test suite; in turn, the full test suite is used as part of the development team's periodic build and test cycle.

At Digital, when the development team decides to freeze the code for a base level, it must test and review the base level before creating a DEC/CMS class. The DEC/CMS class will associate all the source modules for easy access. To build distribution kits of the media, the team uses the base-level class. Base-level development continues if the product is not yet complete, or ends if the DEC/CMS class represents the final base level for release.

7.1 Levels of Testing

The complexity of the environment within which a team tests the code determines the level of testing that is required. The two levels of testing are:

- Unit testing
- Integrated testing

Unit testing takes place on code that constitutes the simplest environment. In unit testing, engineers test a unit of code, such as a subprogram, subroutine, internal procedure, or module before it becomes part of a larger procedure.

Integrated testing takes place on code that constitutes a progressively more complex environment as the individual units are combined into larger functional components. More than one level of integrated testing may be needed to test all functional components of a software product.

Figure 7–1: Code Testing Process

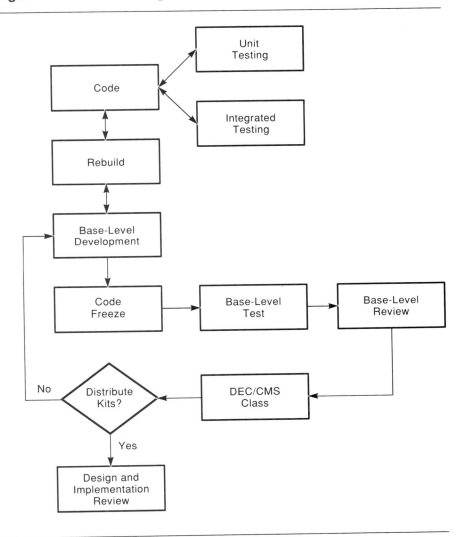

For example, a unit test for an accounts receivable module of a business accounting package might determine whether the module correctly calculates the total for a sale, including any taxes, to a customer. Similarly, an integrated test might determine whether the items sold are subtracted in the inventory module of the business accounting package.

In Figure 7–2, level 1 represents unit testing, and levels 2 and 3 represent integrated testing.

Figure 7–2: Unit and Integrated Levels of Testing

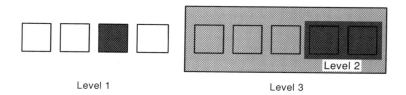

Level 1   Level 3

7.1.1 Unit Testing

Thorough unit testing is good coding practice. Typically, in unit testing a specific test is written or an existing test modified for a unit of code.

After writing a test, Digital developers use the VAX Performance and Coverage Analyzer (VAX PCA) together with the DEC/Test Manager to see how effectively the test covers the code. If the DEC/Test Manager indicates a high percentage of code is covered, the team can have confidence that the test is a valid indicator of correctness. On the other hand, if the DEC/Test Manager indicates that a low percentage of code is covered by the test, the test is modified or augmented.

For instance, a team whose tests cover 85 percent (suggested minimum) of the product's code paths can be more confident that their tests are measuring the correctness of the product than a team whose test coverage is only 68 percent. However, as the coverage values for the application increase, the team must trade off the cost of developing new and more comprehensive tests against the cost of fixing an otherwise undiscovered error. The type of application being developed also has a large effect on this judgment.

7.1.2 Integrated Testing

The approach to integrated testing preferred at Digital is called incremental testing. With this approach, testing begins with a single unit. Testing continues as more units are added to the original unit. Each unit is thoroughly tested before it is included in the integrated testing process. At each level, errors are corrected before going on to the next level. At the last step, testing the units in combination, the entire procedure should work correctly.

Incremental testing helps find the following types of errors:

- Problems with the calling interface between units
- Incorrect assumptions about what values are returned and which units they are returned to
- Unexpected transfer of control between units

Incremental testing has many advantages: the entire procedure need not be complete to begin integrated testing. Debugging is simplified because modules and interfaces can be tested as the system grows. In addition, programming errors in the interfaces and incorrect assumptions between units surface at an early stage. Finally, because existing units are retested as new units are added to the test set, undesirable or unexpected interactions among code units are more likely to be detected.

7.2 Types of Tests

The unit and integrated tests are generally classified as "white box" or "black box." Table 7–1 shows some characteristics of white box tests and black box tests.

Table 7–1:   White Box Tests and Black Box Tests

White Box Tests	Black Box Tests
Primarily used for unit testing	Primarily used for integrated testing
Can be written in the design phase only if documents are quite detailed	Can be written based on the requirements, specifications, and design documents; usually used for functional tests
Used to examine how the results were achieved at the code path level	Used to examine whether a procedure produces the expected results without concern for the underlying code

7.2.1   White Box Tests

White box tests examine the internal workings of the code, that is, the individual lines of code. A set of test data should test each statement, decision, and condition. If a set of test data fails to do so, sections of code that contain errors might be skipped. For example, compound or nested decisions may have many possible branches of code; the test data needs multiple values to force the execution of these branches.

Digital engineers find the VAX Performance and Coverage Analyzer (VAX PCA) to be particularly useful for white box tests. When used with the VAX DEC/Test Manager, VAX PCA measures test coverage. The coverage analysis takes two forms:

- Percentage of total coverage: Indicates how much of the code was executed by the test data.

- Individual source line coverage: Shows which lines of code were executed by the test data.

VAX PCA provides a way to mark code as acceptably not covered. This method allows portions of the code to be bypassed during testing. These portions are typically not testable or the conditions cannot be reproduced. Coverage analysis considers these conditions when calculating coverage percentages.

7.2.2   Black Box Tests

Black box tests measure whether the procedure can produce the predicted results for particular input values. A command procedure is written that repetitively executes the tested procedure with different input values.

The input values come from the following categories:

- Expected inputs
- Boundary values
- Illegal values

7.3   Testing and Design

The development team must plan for testing when they create an application's design. The team should recognize that the product eventually will be tested for validity and consistency. The verification process uses standard testing procedures (for example, regression testing) that the team can plan for.

7.3.1   Design Considerations

The design work generally reveals potential problems such as running out of disk space or a possible failure of system services. If such problems cannot be "designed out" of the system, having a record of them can be valuable when the team prepares its tests.

The team writes the set of functional validation tests during preliminary design to ensure that the tests measure the functions the software is to perform. If the team writes the tests after the code is written, their knowledge of the code may affect the way they write the tests. This approach diminishes the objectivity of the test and the value of the results.

Functional tests are usually black box tests and can be written based on the requirements, specifications, and design documents. White box tests can be written at the design phase only if the design documents are quite detailed.

A product's successful development is in large part measured against the initial requirements and function list. Therefore, functional tests provide a way to measure the success of the product's development. At Digital, teams usually organize their functional tests on the basis of some characteristic of the application: the command list or perhaps objects manipulated by the application. For example, a test of the VAX DEC/Code Management System (DEC/CMS) would exercise all DEC/CMS commands.

An organization based on objects might validate all the attributes or functions of an element (SHOW ELEMENT, CREATE ELEMENT, DELETE ELEMENT, and so on). By organizing tests this way, it is possible to run a subset of the test system or a DEC/Test Manager group after having changed a particular feature. Note that DEC/Test Manager allows individual tests to be members of more than one group.

When designing tests, the development team examines any product dependencies and whether to take a bottom-up or a top-down approach to testing.

7.3.1.1 Bottom-Up and Top-Down Approaches

Depending on the design of the application, the team takes either a bottom-up or a top-down approach to its integrated testing. For a bottom-up design, the team has an application that develops from primitives—low-level functional units, such as data base routines or file-handling routines that form the working base of the application. As the application develops, the low-levels units are combined into larger components. The higher-level combinations of units execute and make use of the primitives to produce the functions of the application. At the highest level, the user interface drives the lower levels of the application.

To carry out tests on a bottom-up design, it is necessary to test the primitives before higher levels of code exist. For this task, driver programs must be written to execute the primitives by calling the routines. In this way unit testing can begin, followed by integrated testing as the application grows. The driver programs are used only until the higher-level code is written.

A top-down design creates a different set of circumstances for testing. A top-down design starts with major functions, such as interface routines or calling routines. These high-level units exist before the primitives. After it is clear how they work together, the lower-level functions are designed. The primitives will ultimately be needed to carry out the work.

For top-down designs, dead-end units or "stubs" are created that return dummy values to the higher-level calling routine. In this way, unit testing can be carried out at higher levels and progress downward to the lower levels as the application develops.

7.3.1.2 Product Dependencies

In designing tests, Digital's developers also consider a set of test data that verify all levels of a product's dependencies on other products. Tests that validate relationships between one product's components and another product's components help development teams discover problems when changes among dependent products occur. The following list contains examples of dependencies for which development teams might design validation tests:

- Operating system dependencies
- Hardware-specific dependencies
- Prerequisite products
- Optional products
- User interfaces
- International layers (translation dependencies)

7.3.2 Regression Testing

Regression testing is the most common technique for evaluating test results. In regression testing, established software tests are run (white box or black box) and the results compared with the successful results from previous test runs. If the new results do not conform to the previously verified results, the software being tested may contain errors. If errors do exist, the software is said to have "regressed." Thus, regression testing ensures that a program runs consistently and that new features do not affect the correct execution of previously tested features.

This is a typical sequence of steps used in regression testing:

1. Write test scripts (command procedures or interactive session records) to test the software.

2. Organize the tests and create a mechanism that lets the team readily access the tests as needed.

3. Run the tests.

4. Examine the test results.

   a. Compare the results of each test to the expected results. Note any differences between the expected and actual results.

   b. For incorrect test output, revise the program code to correct the problem. Repeat steps 3 and 4 until the test output is correct.

   c. Save the correct output as the validated test results.

5. Repeat steps 3 and 4 whenever the program is modified.

   a. If the current and validated test results match, the program being tested is working as expected.

   b. If unexpected changes are found in the test results, the program being tested may contain errors. Correct the program and rerun the tests whose results did not match. Repeat this cycle until all results are valid. For future test runs, use these validated test results as references against which to compare the current test results.

Digital's engineers use the VAX DEC/Test Manager for organizing software regression tests and test results. The DEC/Test Manager automates steps 2 through 4, although engineers must still create the tests manually. Figure 7–3 shows the steps used in regression testing, with those steps the DEC/Test Manager automates indicated in the outlined area.

Here is a typical sequence of steps for using the DEC/Test Manager to perform regression testing:

1. Create tests by writing test scripts to test the software.

2. Set up a DEC/Test Manager system.

   a. Create a DEC/Test Manager library.

Figure 7–3: DEC/Test Manager and Regression Testing

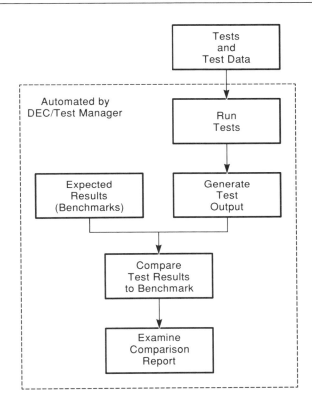

b. Identify each test and its related files to the DEC/Test Manager.

c. Categorize the tests, if desired, by placing them in groups.

3. Run the tests.

a. Use the DEC/Test Manager to collect the test or set of tests that will be run. (DEC/Test Manager can fetch tests directly from a DEC/CMS library.)

b. Run the collection of tests either interactively or in batch mode.

4. Compare the current test results with the expected results for each test. After the test results from the first run have been examined and validated, the DEC/Test Manager will automatically compare new test results with the validated results for each test and record any differences in a differences file.

5. Examine the test results. The DEC/Test Manager provides an interactive subsystem that allows access to test results immediately. To simplify retesting, the DEC/Test Manager also allows engineers to update or create benchmark files that group all tests that produce incorrect results.

6. Repeat steps 3 through 5 whenever you modify the program or add new code.

The DEC/Test Manager simplifies the testing process, thereby increasing the likelihood that all team members will test the application consistently. The DEC/Test Manager can provide the information to answer questions such as the following:

- Who added a specific test?
- Who revised the test set and when?
- How often is the test set run?
- What are the variables used for?

To set up a test system, the engineers create tests and store the test descriptions in a DEC/Test Manager library to identify the tests and their associated files to the DEC/Test Manager. A test description consists of a series of fields whose contents point to files and other information needed to run the test. The core of the test description is the template file. For tests that are not interactive, the template file is a DCL command file created to run a specified test; for interactive tests, the DEC/Test Manager automatically creates a template file when the interactive terminal session is recorded.

You can use the VAX Language-Sensitive Editor (LSE) to create template files more easily. LSE allows engineers to write generalized templates for languages not supported by Digital. They can also write LSE templates for the DEC/Test Manager files if they have several tests that share common characteristics. This approach makes it easier to create and use tests.

For more information on the DEC/Test Manager, see Section 2.1.4.

While regression testing enables the development team to be certain that successive versions of the software yield consistent test results, the team also conducts performance testing to ensure that the software performs its functions correctly.

7.4 Performance Testing

Performance testing helps ensure that a product performs its functions at the required speed. Planning for performance testing starts at the beginning of the project when product goals and requirements are defined. Performance testing is a part of the product's initial engineering plan.

Insofar as possible, the development team states the performance requirements in measurable terms. When this is difficult, the product requirements document provides some guidance as to the importance of the product's performance. Increasingly, performance may affect a product's acceptance in the marketplace. The performance of competing products, therefore, can serve as comparative benchmarks.

The development team can approach performance testing in one of three ways.

1. The team can design for performance. Techniques such as modeling and prototyping help to assess the application's performance. Techniques for validating designs help produce an application design that can enhance performance.

2. The team can test performance during development. This approach entails testing performance at the unit level. The team writes tests and establishes performance benchmarks for each unit tested. The drawback to this approach is the significant time and effort required.

3. The development team can test the performance of the finished product. This approach also requires tests and benchmarks. However, the team creates the tests and benchmarks only for the full application. For this reason, it is more practical than testing during development.

Assuming that the team chooses the third approach, the engineers must first create the tests and benchmarks. This step is difficult because it entails translating information from the requirements and specification stages into tests and benchmarks that are specific to individual products. Without meaningful benchmarks, however, performance testing serves little purpose.

7.4.1 Running Regression Tests

Once the team establishes performance criteria for the product, it can run appropriate regression tests. As mentioned earlier in this chapter, the DEC/Test Manager can help the team manage the tests and evaluate the results. Because the DEC/Test Manager is a consistency-testing tool, the development team has to write a filter for tests that collect VMS accounting data at logout. Typical information includes CPU time, elapsed time, and page fault data. To be meaningful, the tests need to be run consistently, that is, on the same class of equipment under the same conditions. The team must ensure that these conditions exist.

When the tests are run, the DEC/Test Manager can compare benchmarks automatically with the data collected. This type of performance testing is suitable for applications that are batch-intensive. The DEC/Test Manager cannot measure human interface aspects of performance. This is best addressed by human factors testing. (See Section 4.4 for information on human interface design.)

7.4.2 Resolving Performance Problems

Experience has shown that it is difficult for engineers to intuitively determine where the greatest performance problems occur in their programs. The VAX Performance and Coverage Analyzer (VAX PCA) can be extremely helpful in locating the problem in the source code.

If the regression testing shows that the application no longer compares favorably with the established benchmarks, VAX PCA can be used to help improve performance. Figure 7–4 shows where VAX PCA fits in the performance testing process.

Figure 7–4: Performance Test Process

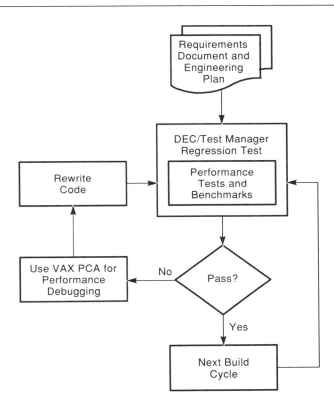

In effect, VAX PCA functions as a performance debugger, quickly identifying sections of code that consume the largest portions of performance time. Once the bottlenecks are located, the code and its algorithms can be rewritten.

VAX PCA can also help when a performance problem occurs during field test. A performance problem in this sense does not reflect a section of code whose logic fails to work; rather, it reflects a section of code that performs inefficiently, perhaps in special circumstances. Examples of this type of problem include hidden N^2 algorithms, code that is too general, or code that is poorly designed.

VAX PCA can be used in much the same way to solve both types of performance problems. However, note that reacting to performance problems that become apparent during field test is not the same as developing a strategy of performance testing against benchmarks.

7.5 Summary of Testing Guidelines

This section summarizes the key guidelines covered in previous sections of this chapter.

Error Testing

- Plan the application's design with testing in mind.
- Plan the testing itself as early as possible.
- Use black and white box tests to exercise the code.
- Perform thorough unit testing before beginning integrated testing.
- Use incremental testing at the integrated level.
- Devise complete functional tests for the product as it matures.
- Devise tests that verify correct error-handling.
- Use regression testing techniques with the DEC/Test Manager to automate and organize the testing process as part of a build/test cycle.
- Use VAX PCA with the DEC/Test Manager to determine the amount of test coverage on tests; rewrite if necessary.
- After any developmental task (error fix, module written, and so on), test the code unit as a unit and then as part of the application test suite before checking the code unit back into the project DEC/CMS code library.

Performance Testing

- Plan performance requirements and specifications for the application.
- Plan tests and benchmarks that define the application's accepted performance.

- Use the DEC/Test Manager to run regression tests that compare performance against established benchmarks as part of the build/test cycle.

- Use VAX PCA to locate sections of code that perform inefficiently; rewrite the sections.

For more information on testing, see the *Guide to Creating VMS Modular Procedures*; see also *The Art of Software Testing* by Glenford J. Myers (see Appendix D).

Chapter 8

Qualification

After a fully functional software product is created, it is time to qualify the product through field tests and to begin steps to release the product to manufacturing. During the qualification phase, the software is in use at selected external field test sites. The development team stays in close contact with these sites, making sure any needed corrections are reflected in the version of the software and documentation to be shipped to the general customer base. In later stages of this test period, source code and documentation are frozen, and final copies of the distribution media and books are prepared.

8.1 Preparing for Field Test

The development team prepared a field test strategy as part of the design and implementation phase of product development. This preliminary field test plan becomes part of the development plan. Thus, it is available to help the team begin identifying appropriate field test sites. Often, the product manager, with help from both the field test administrator and the engineering project leader, takes care of this task.

During design and implementation, the development team works out specific details of the field test process, such as the site configurations and problem reporting mechanisms. This information forms the basis of the field test plan.

The length of an effective field test varies with the product and the sites. Given the time needed to set up, use, and provide feedback, three to four months is generally the minimum field test period. When scheduling a field test, bear in mind that feedback is less likely during holidays and, for universities, at the end of semesters.

Before field test begins, the development team provides the customer with all the information needed to test the product. This information states clearly what the development team expects from the field test sites.

Many of the administrative tasks associated with preparing for field test are the responsibility of the field test administrator; for example, the administrator completes any needed nondisclosure or licensing agreements with the field test site, and distributes the field test kits. The kits are assembled by the development team or release engineer.

The team devises a means of communicating with the field test sites in order to gather feedback and respond to problems. This is often accomplished formally through an online problem report system (see Section 8.1.1), and informally through phone calls and site visits. Before the field test begins, the problem report system is ready to handle the problem reports from field test sites.

8.1.1 Problem Report System

Every development effort needs an effective means of assigning and tracking problem reports throughout the life cycle of the product. Problem reports originate from the following groups and at different times in the product's life cycle:

- From the development group itself—at all stages of the product's development, including unreleased versions
- From internal and external users of field test versions
- From internal and external users of released versions

The ideal setup for problem reporting is a single system that handles all types of problem reports, including reports from field test sites. An online problem report system provides users with an easy way to forward problem reports, concerns, or suggestions to the product developers. Useful features of such a system include the following:

- Online access by both field test sites and developers
- Ease of editing problem report replies
- Standard format of online problem report
- Statistical tracking capabilities
- Flexible display of problem reports in a data base
- Capability to categorize problem reports with keywords (or some counterpart) and status; for example, answered, unanswered, closed, open, and so on

NOTE

Development teams can write their own problem reporting system using Digital's VAX RALLY or VAX DATATRIEVE software in combination with VMS RMS data base files.

Before submitting a product to manufacturing, the development team tries to screen and respond to all problem reports. Typically, one person on the team screens the reports and passes them along to the engineer responsible for the feature in question. Often, development teams set a goal of responding to their problem reports within a short period of time, perhaps two days.

In addition to responding to problem reports, the development team and the product manager meet to discuss the status of each field test site and compare activity to milestones and schedules. The team may need to revise schedules, depending on the quality of the field test. Results of the review meetings are made available to all groups that make up the product team.

8.1.2 Internal Field Test

Before a Digital development team sends test kits to external field test sites, it typically has begun a formal field test within its own group. Internal testing helps to pave the way for external testing. One benefit is that internal tests uncover problems that the team can resolve before undertaking the external test. It is also easier to distribute the product and gain feedback.

For those products that will be sold worldwide, the internal field test includes sites with a comparable worldwide distribution.

8.1.3   Early Evaluation Field Test

One way that Digital developers get feedback on the product before the full-scale external field test is to conduct an early evaluation field test (EEFT). Conducting an EEFT entails testing an application at select customer sites while the product is being developed. Perhaps only 65 percent of the product's features are ready, yet by having selected customers field test the application early, the development team gains valuable information as to whether the product has the right features and is meeting its requirements.

Because the product is not finished, feedback from an EEFT can result in significant redevelopment. Thus, an early evaluation is as much a prototyping effort as it is a developmental engineering step. The likelihood of redevelopment with a consequent impact on the product's schedule requires that management support the EEFT's goals and the development team be prepared for additional work.

Selecting and preparing sites is essential for an EEFT. The sites must understand that the product they will test is unfinished and that they can play a formative role in its development. For this reason, and because of the close interaction between the sites and the development team, it is best to carefully select a small number of sites.

8.2   Conducting the External Field Test

The development team has the following responsibilities during external field test:

- Responding to input from field test sites, including problems and questions
- Informing field test sites of changes to the software
- Participating in reviews of field test sites
- Helping decide whether the field test is meeting its goals, or whether it needs to be modified or extended
- Communicating regularly with other members of the product team
- Providing new field test upgrade kits as required

Members of the development team contact field test sites regularly to provide them with information on changes to the software and to respond to problems and questions.

8.2.1 Fixing Errors

The development team's response to errors that are discovered during field test depends on the severity of the error and when it is discovered. The team fixes minor errors in the code that arise during field test. The modified software is sent back to test sites as part of a field test update kit to verify the changes. The team fixes any minor errors before the code is frozen for production.

The development team must resolve critical errors before submitting the product to manufacturing. Table 8–1 describes how the errors are resolved, which in turn depends on when they are discovered.

Table 8–1: Resolution of Critical Errors

If the error is discovered after the development team...	The development team must...
Sends out a field test upgrade kit to the field (see Section 8.2.2)	Analyze and solve the problem, make the change, and test the software. Testing helps validate the solution and may detect regressive effects elsewhere in the software.
Reviews and signs off the product documentation (assuming the error affects the documentation)	Repeat the final verification period to fix the documentation. This usually means delaying submission to manufacturing.
Submits the product to manufacturing. This creates the most serious problem.	Withdraw the product from manufacturing and repeat the entire verification procedure.

8.2.2 Final Verification: Field Test Upgrade Kits

Before the field test period ends, the development team sends upgrade kits to the field test sites. An upgrade kit is submitted as the final version of the software and the documentation, both of which will eventually be sent to manufacturing.

This portion of the field test makes up the final verification of the product. The project team sends out the upgrade kit to make sure there are no undetected problems.

8.3 Closing the Field Test

The field test plan states how long the field test will last and the criteria for ending it. Conditions such as the quality of the field test results or the severity of the software problem can force the development team to adjust the field test schedule. The decision to extend or close the field test rests with the development team, which relies on recommendations from the product team.

8.3.1 Manufacturing Verification

After the field test is completed, the development team meets the following list of criteria to verify that the product is ready for manufacturing:

- Testing is complete and all known problems in the code and documentation have been corrected.
- The code is frozen.
- All software masters have been built and submitted to manufacturing.
- The final draft of all documentation is available, including installation and installation verification procedures.

The development team may add its own criteria to this list. It also includes time in the development schedule to verify that the product meets all the criteria.

To ensure that a stable product is delivered to manufacturing, all of Digital's software products also meet the following final checks before being submitted to manufacturing:

- The product can be installed according to the installation documentation.
- All demonstration programs and the distribution kit, including documentation, are complete and accurate.
- All product documents (manuals, descriptions, and release notes) are ready for the printer.
- The final verification of the product in its intended market environment is complete.
- The development team has recorded and submitted for correction all problems discovered during the product's final verification (after the upgrade kit is sent out).
- The development team has corrected and verified errors that do not affect the product's documentation.

When all checks are complete, the product is ready to be signed off by all participants.

8.3.2 Field Test Reports

During the field test, the development team gets a great deal of feedback from the test sites. This feedback is compiled into a report on the field test results. The report organizes the data from the field test sites, including the following types of information:

- Test results
- Problems (classified by priority) encountered by the test sites
- Responses to these problems
- Survey results of user perceptions
- Polling results
- Complications during testing

Typically, the project's field test administrator helps organize and consolidate this information, for example, by statistically analyzing the data.

8.3.3 Product Evaluation Report

The product evaluation report represents the development team's evaluation as to whether the product is ready to ship to customers. After analyzing key sections of the field test results to substantiate its evaluation, the development team makes the product evaluation report available to the development supervisor and other members of the product team.

The product evaluation report contains a condensed analysis of all the testing and product evaluation that has been carried out. This includes field test data, regression testing, software product description verification, and a serviceability evaluation report. The product evaluation report is agreed to by the entire product team, and it includes these items:

- Clearly stated test results and evaluations compared to each goal, capability, and external characteristic as stated in the product specification.
- A statement of the product's status compared to the defined software manufacturing submission criteria for the product. This statement shows that the product meets the criteria for submission to manufacturing (see Section 8.3.1).
- A statement of test and evaluation results compared to the goals and capabilities defined in the customer services plan, the training plan, and the software manufacturing plan.

8.3.4 Release Notes

Release notes provide a way to document significant changes to the product since the last release and/or any last-minute changes that the team could not include in the standard documentation. The following items might be included in release notes:

- Code errors fixed before shipping
- Known code errors or restrictions
- Changes from last release
- Documentation changes and omissions

Release notes do not contain information that is better documented elsewhere, such as information on new features and installation procedure instructions.

Chapter 9

Maintenance

Various studies have shown that from 60 to 70 percent of the cost of software is incurred during maintenance.[1] Although this percentage varies considerably from project to project, it does indicate that maintenance accounts for a significant portion of engineering resources throughout the life cycle of a software product.

Therefore, planning how to minimize maintenance costs is an ongoing concern. This chapter highlights the planning required to address maintenance concerns in all phases of software development.

Depending on the status of a product, maintenance tasks vary, but these tasks are typical:

- Eliminating errors in the application
- Enhancing the application in response to customer feedback
- Solving regression problems (for example, the application does not work on a particular system)
- Testing the application on new processors, both previous versions in the field and new development versions
- Updating documentation to reflect changes in the application
- Analyzing statistics and metrics collected from customers using the product

---

[1] *Guidance on Software Maintenance*. NBS Special Publication 500-106. National Bureau of Standards, 1983.

9.1 Planning for Maintenance

The best way to reduce maintenance work is to minimize the avoidable errors in the application. The farther along a product is in its development cycle, the higher the cost of fixing errors. Table 9–1 compares the costs of fixing problems at various times in the development cycle.

Table 9–1: Relative Costs of Fixing Software Errors

Time When Fixed	Cost Multiplier
During design phase	1
During coding phase	1.5
Just before base-level test	10
During base-level test	60
During field test	100

The maintenance team accomplishes its work more easily if development is carried out with maintenance in mind. This is particularly important because often the maintenance team is made up of engineers who did not participate in the original development work. If the development team uses the tools and follows the procedures described in the previous chapters, the development process is easier for everyone. It is during maintenance, however, that these procedures really show their worth.

Without an effective set of work procedures, the maintenance team will find itself with a series of potential problems, for example:

- It may not be able to reproduce code in the field.
- It may not know what tests were run and where the tests are stored.
- It may not be able to review old versions of code.
- It may not update product specifications to reflect changes in code or features.

9.2 Maintenance Procedures

This section emphasizes software development procedures that can make software maintenance tasks easier and less costly:

- Project environment
- Project conventions
- Project communication
- Design documentation
- Test plans
- Code conventions
- Build procedures
- Maintenance document
- DEC/CMS libraries
- Problem reports

9.2.1 Project Environment

To set up the project environment, the development team must plan such tasks as file storage, project directory and library structure, and tool use.

Many tasks necessary to facilitate maintenance should have been done during each of the phases already discussed in this guide. Here is a quick review of some of the tools used to carry out these tasks. See Chapter 2, Software Development Tools, for more detail.

- The VAX DEC/Code Management System (DEC/CMS) helps manage and control file storage for both code and documentation. It also facilitates software configuration management.
- The VAX DEC/Module Management System (DEC/MMS) can control, in conjunction with DEC/CMS, the build process for the application; DEC/MMS is particularly useful if the project has not already developed extensive build procedures for previous versions.
- The VAX DEC/Test Manager helps organize and run project tests.
- The VAX Language-Sensitive Editor (LSE) simplifies coding conventions, source control, compilations, and editing and debugging tasks.

- The VAX Source Code Analyzer (VAX SCA) provides cross-referencing and static analysis among an application's modules. It is particularly useful for helping new engineers become familiar with an application's code.
- The VAX Performance and Coverage Analyzer (VAX PCA) is an aid for performance debugging.
- The VMS Debugger debugs code.
- VAX SCAN writes filters, extractors, and translators.
- VAX Notes makes many kinds of project communication easier across the network.

In addition to these tools, the development team needs to establish a problem-reporting mechanism to handle problem reports over the life cycle of the product. This mechanism has features to both assign and track problems reported with the software. Without such a mechanism in place, the maintenance tasks will be much more difficult.

The tools the team chooses will affect the directory and library structure for the project. The directory structure should fulfill three purposes:

1. Provide a comprehensive and adequate file storage hierarchy
2. Provide the necessary storage libraries for specific tools (for example, DEC/CMS, VAX SCA, and DEC/Test Manager libraries)
3. Have a structure that is readily understandable and accessible to its users

A Methodology for Software Development Using VMS Tools provides useful examples of how to set up a project's directories and libraries to maximize the use of Digital's software development tools.

Once the team has designed its directory structure, team members typically use logical names to speed access to particular directories and to provide more generic specifications. *A Methodology for Software Development Using VMS Tools* has examples of logical names as well.

9.2.2 Project Conventions

When setting up the directory hierarchy, team members agree on conventions for the project. For example:

- Specification formats
- Design formats
- Naming conventions for files, modules, routines, and tests
- Conventions for DEC/CMS and DEC/Test Manager remarks that are logged in the respective tool's history file
- Comment formats for module and routine prefaces
- Test headers (similar to module headers) that provide a test's name, function, and any special requirements for running the tests

Previous chapters of this book describe how to establish such standards, for example, by using LSE templates to enforce coding conventions (see Chapter 6, Coding Guidelines for Implementation).

By agreeing on these standards early in the project and adhering to them throughout, the team avoids confusion and conflict. An added benefit is that standards provide a consistent framework for new team members, enabling them to quickly learn about the project. Chapter 4, Planning and Preliminary Design, Chapter 6, Coding Guidelines for Implementation, and Chapter 7, The Testing Process, contain specific information on relevant standards.

Coding Conventions

As explained in Chapter 6, development teams can use LSE to format code consistently. Code that is formatted consistently is easier to read, benefiting not only team members, but also engineers who may maintain or update the application in the future. The use of LSE and regular code reviews (described in Section 6.5) promote coding consistency.

Naming Conventions

Adhering to naming conventions also helps both the development and maintenance teams. Naming conventions for modules, routines, and variables provide a number of benefits:

- Faster identification of code elements
- Easier access to files and directories using wildcard characters
- Faster learning by engineers new to a project
- Faster work with the VMS Debugger
- Easier maintenance of the software

See Section 6.4 and the *Guide to Creating VMS Modular Procedures* for detailed information on naming conventions.

Conventions for DEC/CMS and DEC/Test Manager Remarks

Another convention that Digital developers follow concerns the information put in the remarks of tools, notably DEC/CMS and DEC/Test Manager. These remarks should provide useful information, such as a clear problem description. The engineers can then reference the module and the routines that were modified.

Furthermore, the problem, its cause, and the number of the associated report can be duplicated in the source code using the modification history comments (see Section 6.1.3.1). The modification history comments specify which tests were run to check the effects of the code changes. Engineers can track this information and cross-reference from the report numbers to the code. This supplementary knowledge helps engineers to more quickly understand the code.

9.2.3 Project Communication

Without communication, members of the team can easily lose track of what other team members are doing. A number of problems can result:

- Team members may duplicate effort.
- Team members may miss opportunities to make use of reusable code.
- The code design may not be truly modular.
- Modules developed by different team members may not work together.

Several mechanisms can help to reduce these problems.

Project Account

To help make information easily accessible to all team members, the team can set up a project account to receive all project-related MAIL messages. This account can also store the results of project builds and other relevant files, and be accessible to the entire team.

Project Conferences

VAX Notes can help a team organize many of its information-handling tasks. Typical project needs met by VAX Notes include the following:

- A suggestion box as an ongoing "wish list" to plan for the next release of the product
- A forum to keep up-to-date on issues and answers for customers and internal users
- A place for public announcements, such as the availability of new versions of software

Project Meetings

Project meetings need to be held frequently enough to maintain adequate communication within the project; once a week is appropriate for many teams. All members need to stay up-to-date on all the project work. The information they gain from the project meeting feeds back into the development work, generating a better quality product.

Often, project meetings serve as review forums to help verify that team members are following code, design, and specification conventions. These reviews can also help transfer knowledge. For example, designers may not always implement their own designs. Design reviews can help to ensure that the design is clear and understandable to the engineer assigned the task of implementing the design. (Section 4.5 contains more information on design reviews; Section 6.5 has more information on code reviews.)

9.2.4 Design Documentation

The design documentation provides a record of major design decisions, for example:

- Alternatives not taken and why
- Future enhancements, including the range of possibilities and ideas considered
- Failings or limitations of outside software and hardware, for example, operating system version requirements and emulator incompatibilities

The team can use an LSE design template to set up consistent means of recording this type of information. They can refer to this information when they make changes to the code.

Another task that helps with maintenance is reviewing (usually during team meetings) the correlation between the specifications and the designs. The team checks to see that all developers have designed those features that meet the application's requirements and specifications.

See Section 4.5 for more information on design reviews.

9.2.5 Test Plans

As they are designing an application, the team also plans their tests. Although pieces of the software may not be running, the team is likely to be familiar with the software design and with any problems that may occur during its implementation. When designing the application, engineers can create a DEC/Test Manager test stored in the test system. In writing this test, they need to keep in mind the potential problems uncovered during design. When a piece of running software becomes available, the team can refer to the test. This approach helps ensure that design knowledge is preserved.

At the design stage the team considers its white box and black box testing strategy (see Section 7.2.2 and Section 7.2.1). The project team must decide how much of each kind of testing will be done and must determine an integration strategy for testing the design's coded implementation.

9.2.6   Code Conventions

When writing code, engineers need to be concerned with more than efficient algorithms. Maintaining the code is easier if it is formatted consistently, commented clearly, and reviewed for its adherence to project standards.

Using LSE

Projects that use LSE can enforce coding standards effectively for formatting and use. The consistency provided by LSE greatly aids maintainers as they attempt to modify code. An added benefit of LSE is its capacity to provide online language help. LSE templates make it much easier to fill in language constructs accurately, particularly in those instances when an engineer is less familiar with the construct. By expanding the LSE placeholders, an engineer gains additional language information. In effect, engineers can use LSE as a learning aid while producing code for their application.

Commenting

As the coding progresses, engineers make many design decisions. Comments associated with the source code provide one of the best ways for other team members to understand these design decisions and to understand the limitations of the code. Engineers can document potential problem areas at this same level in the code. They can use LSE templates to ensure that comments are entered in a consistent format.

Reviews

Regular code reviews enable the team to check for a number of characteristics important for maintenance. The team reviews for code consistency and adherence to project standards. Reviews ensure that the code reflects the current requirements, specifications, and designs. Throughout the development cycle, team members must be able to trace requirements to implemented code. This process is critical both to the quality of the application and to changing or enhancing the application.

9.2.7 Build Procedures

The team's build procedures accomplish a number of tasks to optimize maintenance:

- Building base levels accurately
- Running and reviewing tests with major builds
- Developing base levels so that ongoing work continues while earlier versions or variants are accessible
- Recording or documenting build procedures so that engineers can re-create important base levels

Digital's DEC/Module Management System (DEC/MMS) provides a number of advantages that make it a popular choice among Digital engineers for building applications, particularly for new projects. DEC/MMS is partially integrated with DEC/CMS, so it can pull modules directly from DEC/CMS during builds. Furthermore, DEC/MMS understands DEC/CMS classes. As a result, a development team can save previous base levels in DEC/CMS as multiple unique classes. These DEC/CMS class names, when properly designated to DEC/MMS, cause it to rebuild a previous version using only the files and elements related to that version. Rebuilds of previous versions are particularly useful during maintenance when multiple versions may be in the hands of customers while the development team is working on new variant development.

A useful feature of DEC/MMS is the description file, which contains the relationships among the modules in an application. The description file serves as a useful record of the application's structure to maintainers. Engineers can check any changes or additions to modules against the description file. This permanent record removes much of the confusion from build procedures during maintenance.

Engineers create and run tests in parallel with their coding. Coding is not considered finished until tests with verified coverage exist. The tests are run and reviewed with each build to catch problems as soon as possible to reduce costs. Chapter 7, The Testing Process, contains more information on testing.

9.2.8 Maintenance Document

The development team prepares a maintenance document, which provides the maintenance team with key information about the software system so that changes can be made with a minimum of difficulty. It contains information such as the following:

- The location of all the relevant documents for the project, for example, design documents in a DEC/CMS library
- Header comments for the source code
- Location of the code in the executable file
- Tools used during development, including version numbers

Engineers can create a maintenance document using a series of commands that retrieve and format all the related information from project storage disks. They can then edit the resulting document. Alternatively, they can write the information in the form of DIGITAL Standard Runoff (DSR) or VAX DOCUMENT files, which can be processed to generate a formatted document.

To be useful, maintenance documents must accurately reflect the current state of the project. If developers fail to update project documents over the development life cycle of the product, maintenance documents have limited value.

The maintenance document can also be useful if a product is being developed for international markets. In addition to basic project information, maintainers might include information on how the design of the product affects efforts to localize the product for a particular country. This section of the document might describe which parts of the application need to be changed to support languages other than English. It might also detail how the modular design of the application facilitates the changes.

9.2.9 DEC/CMS Libraries

Digital's DEC/Code Management System (DEC/CMS) software contains elements and classes that can help organize and relate specification and design stages. In addition, DEC/CMS classes and groups can save time during maintenance.

For example, Figure 9–1 shows a DEC/CMS code library with two groups, each containing two elements. The groups, designated in this example as the FORTRAN group and the Pascal group, classify functions with a common purpose. Engineers, either during implementation or maintenance, can reserve the FORTRAN group to access all the FORTRAN elements rather than specifying each element individually. This type of organization saves time, particularly in fixing an error during maintenance.

Figure 9–1: Use of DEC/CMS Groups for Maintenance

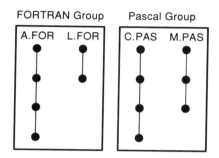

9.2.10 Problem Reports

When a problem report comes in, a maintainer needs to know how the project area is laid out. That is why, during the early phases of development, the team considers the future needs for maintenance when designing the project storage areas and the application. The storage areas should provide easy access to specifications, designs, and source code.

Once the system is fully accessible, the following series of steps can be taken to isolate and correct problems:

1. Build the system, perhaps by using DEC/MMS, to pull the modules from DEC/CMS using the class name.
2. Locate the user's problem using the VMS Debugger, VAX SCA, and LSE.
3. Reserve a modifiable source module directly from DEC/CMS using LSE.
4. Edit the source code using LSE and following the existing formatting conventions in the code.
5. Modify the associated requirements, specifications, design, and user documentation as necessary; future maintainers thus have complete information on any change.
6. Build the local system using modified files linked against the global system.
7. Add any tests to the test system that check the modified code.
8. Verify the code path coverage on the new tests.
9. Replace the reserved modules in the DEC/CMS code library.
10. Create a new DEC/CMS class containing the code that eliminates the problem; the modified code should be on a variant line of descent in the DEC/CMS library.
11. Merge variant code into the next maintenance release of the software.
12. Answer the original problem report.

The following sections discuss how to use the development tools and procedures to perform these tasks.

Making the Changes

Figure 9–2 shows how DEC/CMS helps engineers continue development work on Version 2.0 while eliminating problems from Version 1.0, which in this case is stored as a DEC/CMS class. The problems found in Version 1.0 are corrected on a variant line of descent, which will be merged back into a subsequent release.

Figure 9–2: Variant Development

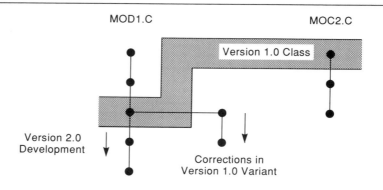

Having multiple DEC/CMS libraries can make it easier to trace the code back to its designs, specifications, and requirements. For instance, Figure 9–3 shows multiple DEC/CMS libraries for the requirements documents, specifications, design documents, tests, and source code. By using the same class name for all files and elements associated with a specific version, maintainers can quickly pull out all files related to that version. Thus, the information is readily available and maintainers can easily modify the various documents if a coding change is made. Finally, DEC/CMS records all the changes in the form of a history record.

Testing the Changes

After locating and correcting the error, the maintenance engineers must relink to build the image. The image must then be tested to ensure that the code fix has not caused some other part of the application to stop functioning properly. The VAX DEC/Test Manager is useful for running the appropriate regression tests. (See Section 7.3.2 for more information on regression testing.)

Figure 9–3: Multiple DEC/CMS Libraries

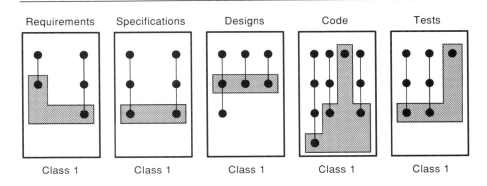

Requirements	Specifications	Designs	Code	Tests
Class 1	Class 1	Class 1	Class 1	Class 1

This is the stage where planning the test system saves time. The test set must be the one that corresponds to the product in the field, in this case, the version that is the source of the error report. This test set must be available to the maintainers, even though new development work may be in progress.

To speed up the testing process, engineers can use the group feature of DEC/Test Manager that allows them to run a subset of tests. This subset relates to the error fixed in the source code. For example, engineers may run the data base subset of tests in a local work area. If no problems occur for the smaller subset, they may run the full system test for this version of the product. If the error is a small one, running the subset of tests may be sufficient.

Another feature of DEC/Test Manager that helps during maintenance is the use of benchmark and template directories. Librarywide defaults can be specified for both the benchmark directory and the template directory. The default directories represent the set of tests and corresponding benchmarks that the development team accesses most often, for example, a new version of the application under development.

These same default directories can be overridden during a DEC/Test Manager test collection. Overriding the defaults is useful when one maintenance version is in the field and a different maintenance version is undergoing development. In a typical maintenance scenario, a problem report for Version 1.1 comes in. In response to the report, maintainers initiate a DEC/Test Manager test collection by specifying a directory with Version 1.1 tests and their corresponding benchmarks. The Version 1.1 tests are run and compared to the valid Version 1.1 benchmarks.

The same tests could be running for Version 1.2; that is, Version 1.2 still uses the same test scripts to test the application. However, in the case of a reported error in Version 1.1, the maintainer initiates the DEC/Test Manager test collection by specifying a different directory for the benchmarks: Version 1.1 benchmarks. Although there would be only one template set and one test set for Versions 1.1 and 1.2, DEC/Test Manager would use different directories for the benchmarks.

The integration of DEC/CMS with DEC/Test Manager simplifies the process of running tests for previous versions. If tests and benchmarks for maintenance Version 1.1 are stored in a DEC/CMS class, maintainers can run them on the debugged Version 1.1. The tests and benchmarks for Version 1.2 or Version 2.0 have separate DEC/CMS classes and thus are not affected.

If the tests are new or produce different results because of the change to the code, engineers must update the benchmarks. The new test result files become the new benchmarks and are stored in the DEC/CMS library for test benchmarks. DEC/Test Manager does this automatically when updated. Furthermore, both DEC/CMS and DEC/Test Manager provide a history of the changes.

Engineers check any new tests for code path coverage by using DEC/Test Manager and VAX PCA together. See Section 7.2.1 for more information.

Performance Debugging

If the problem reported constitutes a performance weakness, the team can consider using VAX PCA to find routines and lines of code that consume the most time. It can then attempt to code the problem sections again. Refer to Section 7.4 for more information on performance debugging.

9.3   Software Development Productivity

The driving force behind efforts to improve productivity is the demand of the market for reliable software products. At the same time, software applications have become more complex, which makes the task of delivering reliable applications more difficult. Productivity metrics can help a team achieve greater development productivity.

9.3.1   Productivity Metrics

During a project's life cycle, the development team is likely to be interested in answers to the following types of questions:

- Has the product's defect rate gone down?
- What tools are being used and to what effect?
- What are the reasons for rework?
- Are problem reports under control?
- Is the schedule reasonable?

Collecting and evaluating software metrics can provide the answers.

The productivity of software development can be assessed in terms of the people, the process, and the resulting software system.

- Engineering productivity entails such issues as how much work developers do in a unit of time, their morale, the effect of training, and trade-offs between creativity and discipline.
- To improve the productivity of the process, teams can investigate what they can automate, the costs of automation, and how to minimize obstacles and delays.
- The software system itself can be examined for its quality, reliability, error rate, complexity, and ease of maintenance.

To make improvements in productivity visible, teams must be able to measure it. A software metric can be defined as a quantitative measure that is used to characterize an attribute or quality of a software system or the software development process. The parts of the system (requirements, specifications, code, documentation, tests, and training) can be characterized using a range of attributes:

- Usability
- Maintainability
- Extendibility
- Size
- Defect level
- Performance
- Completeness

The development process can also be characterized by several attributes:

- Cost of development in calendar time, effort, and money
- Predictability of the schedule
- Rate of defect discovery and repair

An appropriate choice of metric attributes depends on such factors as the goals of the metric-collecting process, the questions to be answered, and the computing environment.

9.3.2 Measurement Techniques

Three productivity attributes—size, defects, and cost—can be measured readily and provide a useful range of information about software development efforts. The particular situation and work environment can provide a basis for determining the relative importance of these productivity attributes.

Size

Lines of code (LOC) is a common metric used to measure the size of a product. LOC may include source code plus comment lines. To count LOC, teams must create data collecting procedures. Digital's VAX SCAN, VAX DATATRIEVE, and DCL products can be used for this purpose.

Another measure of product size is documentation size, including number of pages, lines of help text, and lines of error messages.

Defects

The quality of a product can be determined by measuring its defects, typically from first shipment until the version is discontinued. Operationally, defects can be treated as a count of code errors, design errors, or documentation errors, or any combination of the three.

Cost

The cost of the product's development can be counted in person-months. Cost data can be obtained from project accounting records.

Coding Conventions for VAX C

By following coding standards, engineers produce software that is more reliable and easier to maintain and transport. This appendix provides an example of the types of coding guidelines suggested for coding in the VAX C programming language. This appendix represents one suggested C language programming style. Other sources may suggest different C language programming styles.

A.1 Support Tools

Much of Digital's software is intended to run on the VMS operating system, the ULTRIX operating system, or both. Because the VAX C compiler is available on both of these operating systems, its capabilities and restrictions form the basis for the programming guidelines described in this appendix.

Digital also produces software intended to run on other operating systems, for example, MS–DOS or OS/2. A single compiler is unlikely to be available for all these operating systems. Section A.12 discusses portability issues for programs that must run on computer architectures other than VAX architecture.

The VAX C compiler produces high-quality informational, warning, and error messages. Warning and informational messages usually indicate some questionable use of the C language. For this reason, completed C modules should never produce any diagnostic message when compiled.

The VAX C compiler has a /STANDARD=PORTABLE qualifier that causes the compiler to flag nonportable features of the C language. The guidelines in this appendix explicitly prohibit many of these nonportable features. Do not use the qualifier in the initial stages of program development to help identify cases in which a program may not conform to these guidelines. Note that this qualifier often produces informational or warning diagnostics during the compilation of included system header files. For this reason, do not use it when you compile completed C modules.

The VAX Source Code Analyzer has a CHECK CALLS capability that can help you find errors in the number and type of function arguments that the VAX C compiler cannot identify.

The use of LSE templates that support these C programming guidelines can make it much easier for all the engineers on a development team to conform to the guidelines presented in the following sections.

A.2 Module Organization

Divide C programs cleanly into modules of related functions, data, and types. With a small amount of discipline by the programmer, C supports a modular style of programming that is very similar to that of Ada or Modula–2. In this style of programming, a module consists of two parts:

- An external specification that describes the facilities made available by the module
- An implementation part that contains the actual functions and data that match the external specification

In C, the external specification corresponds to a .h file (header file) and the implementation part corresponds to a .c file (C source file). The .h file has the following contents:

- *extern* declarations for all the global variables declared in the .c file
- Function prototypes declared with *extern* for all the global functions declared in the .c file
- Declarations of any types and macros needed to use the *extern* declarations and the function prototypes declared with *extern*

The standard I/O library for C can serve as an example of a well-designed module that has a detailed external interface. Imagine that there is a stdio module that consists of two parts: a *stdio.h* that specifies the external interface of the module and (behind the scenes) a *stdio.c* that implements that specification.

The stdio module exhibits several desirable properties of modules:

- It has a primary function (I/O, in this case).

- It is reusable by many different programs (a useful property that unfortunately cannot be achieved by many modules).

- It specifies its external interface effectively.

The external specification of stdio, *stdio.h*, contains *extern* declarations for the various I/O functions (*fopen, puts, fprintf*, and so on). It contains declarations of the global data from the standard I/O library (*stdin, stdout*, and so on). It even contains types (*FILE*) and constants (*EOF*) made available by stdio.

As in the stdio example, the programming standard described in this appendix requires that each .c file has a corresponding .h file to describe the external interface to that .c file. Any other module that uses the facilities made available by a .c file should include the associated .h file. No .c file should ever contain an *extern* declaration or redeclare a type from another .c file; these should be "imported" by using a #*include* for the .h file. In addition, every .c file should use a #*include* for its associated .h file to allow the compiler to check the external specification of the module against its actual implementation.

If you use this coding standard, the compiler can do a fairly complete job of intermodule type checking at compile time. Every module that uses the facilities of another module does so by including the specification. Thus, as long as that specification is correct, no problems should be caused by objects declared with the wrong type or functions called with the wrong type or number of arguments. Finally, because the external specification is checked against the actual implementation, the specification should be correct.

This checking mechanism is not perfect. It could fail when macros already defined in the file alter the contents of the included .h file. (This type of problem is very rare.)

A.3 Organization of C Source Files

A source file consists of several sections separated by blank lines or a form feed. If a form feed separates sections, it should be the only character on the line.

In general, source files should not exceed 1000 lines because larger files are difficult to edit. One thousand lines represents about 12 to 15 pages of text. No source line should be longer than 80 characters.

All C source files that are not header files should be given the *.c* file type. The following organization applies to source files:

- Use a *module header* comment to describe the contents of the file in a few sentences. This comment is followed by a copyright notice. The prologue describes the purpose of the text in the file and makes clear whether the file contains functions, data definitions, tables, or support code.

- Specify *header files* with the *#include* preprocessor directive. See Section A.4 for more information about header files.

  Do not specify directories in an *#include* directive. Instead, use the proper compiler qualifier to specify the directories for include files at compile time (/INCLUDE on VMS; –I on ULTRIX).

- Specify the *#define*, *typedef*, and *structure* definitions that apply to the file as a whole. See Section A.7 and Section A.8 for more information about these definitions.

- Specify *global data definitions*. The use of global data is strongly discouraged. Using function parameters properly makes global data unnecessary. Where global data is unavoidable, use the following order for definitions:
  1. Any global variables defined in the file
  2. File global (*static*) variables

- Specify *prototypes* for all *static* functions in the file. This list serves as a table of contents for the module and satisfies any requirements for forward declarations of *static* functions. The order of this list corresponds to the order in which the functions are defined in the file.

- Place the *function definitions* last. If the file contains a relatively large number of functions, put them in alphabetical order. If not, higher-level functions should precede lower-level functions; group related functions together. If the file contains the *main( )* function, place it first. Note, however, that if the compiler supports inlining of functions, the definition of any function to be inlined may be required to precede the definitions of functions that invoke it. Separate all function definitions from each other with a form feed.

A.4 Organization of Header Files

Header files are included in other source files during compilation. Some, such as *stdio.h*, are defined system-wide and must be included by any C programs that use the standard I/O library. Others are used within a single program or application.

Like *.c* files, header files consist of several sections separated by blank lines or a form feed. If you use a form feed to separate sections, it should be the only character on the line. All header files should have the *.h* file type.

Header files begin with a *module header* comment that gives the file name followed by a few sentences that tell what is in the file. The copyright notice comes next. This is followed by the prologue, which describes the purpose of the text in the file.

When you include header files, first include all the system header files using the *#include <file.h>* form of the directive. Following the system includes, put in all the application header files using the *#include "file.h"* syntax of the directive.

Avoid nested header files because they may inadvertently be included more than once. This can cause compilation errors because some language constructs, such as *typedef*, must not appear more than once in a single compilation unit. If you must nest header files, you may prevent multiple compilations by using the *#ifndef* preprocessor directive.

For example:

```
#ifndef QUEUE_LOADED
#define QUEUE_LOADED 1

typedef struct
        {
           ...
        } QUEUE_ENTRY;

#endif
```

You should not include nested header files with the *#include "foo.h"* format. The search semantics for this form differ between UNIX and VMS systems. On VMS systems, the VAX C compiler looks first for *foo.h* in the same directory as the top-level C source file. On the other hand, most UNIX compilers (including VAX C/ULTRIX) look first for *foo.h* in the directory in which the immediately including file was found.

Header files should contain any *#define* constants or macros, any *typedef*s, or any *extern* declarations that are shared between two or more modules of an application. Header files should not define (that is, allocate) variables or contain code. If they do, it usually indicates that the code was poorly partitioned between files.

A.5 Comments

There are four general types of comments:

*   The module header comment contains your company's standard software copyright notice, the standard module template, and the module level declarations.
*   All routines should have a standard descriptive comment block.
*   Block comments are narratives describing the purpose of a portion of the program text. (See Section 6.3.4 for formatting examples.)
*   Line comments appear on the same line as the code they describe. (See Section 6.3.4 for formatting examples.)

Do not comment out C code for any purpose. If you need to comment out temporary or debugging code, surround the code with the *#if 0* and *#endif* preprocessor directives on a line by themselves and aligned in column one.

A.6 Naming Conventions

Descriptive names are an important aid to reading and understanding code. Names can describe the semantics of data or functions and may contain tips as to the type of data and where data or functions are defined. The guidelines in this appendix will help you to name things so that other engineers will find it easier to understand the program.

A.6.1 General Considerations

All names should be long enough to be descriptive. Use underscores (_) as boundaries between words or abbreviations in names, for example, *log_error_message( )*.

Never require engineers to notice the slight differences between 1 (a digit), l (lowercase letter), and I (uppercase letter). Another example of a confusing series to avoid is O, Q, and 0. Similarly, avoid the "long constant" identifier. The 1l is a long integer if the second character is the letter L; instead, use 1L.

The C programming language is case-sensitive. All keywords in the language are lowercase. User-defined symbols may be in any case, but case is significant when determining if symbols are equivalent. Case can be used to distinguish different types of names, but you must be careful to avoid ambiguity and errors.

To make them easy to identify, use uppercase for constants, macros, and most type definitions (objects named using the *#define* or *typedef* constructs). For the same reason, use lowercase for local variables, static function names, function parameters, and structure/union members.

The names of external variables and functions may be outside your control. The case of these names will have to conform to their external definitions. Section A.6.3 has a set of guidelines for naming global variables and functions.

A.6.2 Local Names

Variable names must have the same use and meaning throughout a program. Never redefine names in inner blocks or redeclare global names within a function.

Local variables usually have their declaration and use close by. Nevertheless, always provide comments describing use on local variable declarations. It is acceptable to use shorter names for local variables. Standard meaningful names for highly local (temporary) variables include the following:

```
i, j, k      indexes
c, ch        characters
p, cp, bp    pointers
```

A.6.3 Global Names

Follow the rules in this section whenever global names are being made available outside the C application. An example would be a C application that is only a library of general-purpose routines made available to other programs. Another example is a large subsystem (such as a compiler's code generator) that has interfaces to other large subsystems. The rules help when interfacing C code to code written in assembler or Bliss. Those languages lack typing, so engineers must keep in mind the attributes that the following naming scheme describes:

- Global names should have a prefix (PFX) that indicates the facility or application that defines them. For example, an application that has a formally assigned facility code could use it as the prefix. Other applications can choose a suitable abbreviation.

- Global routines that are directly callable by user programs should have the form *PFX_name*. All other global routines should have the form *PFX_name*. Because nonglobal routines lack the PFX_ prefix, they are readily recognizable.

- Global variable and literal names should have the form *PFX_t_ name*, where *t* is the data type according to Table 6–4 in Chapter 6.

- Module names should have the form *PFX_name*. Each source file contains one C module. If the name of the module is *PFX_name*, the name of the source file will be *PFX_name.c*.
- All macros of general utility should be defined in a single file, *PFX_macro.h*, and their names should have the form *_PFX_NAME*.

A portability issue exists in that the dollar sign ($) is not an ANSI C standard identifier character. However, it is a popular extension supported by a large number of C compilers. If the target of your program is not VMS or ULTRIX, you may want to verify that your compiler supports dollar signs in identifiers.

A.6.4   Reserved Names

Common coding practice and the proposed ANSI C standard have reserved many identifiers. In some cases, identifiers are reserved because they are keywords in the various dialects of C. In other cases, identifiers are reserved because they are used for a specific purpose that the engineer is not permitted to interfere with. In still other cases, identifiers are reserved to allow future expansion of the C language or its libraries. Consequently, avoid reserved identifiers when choosing names for the identifiers in your program.

The keywords of the C language are reserved. In general, the compiler flags accidental uses of a keyword as a user identifier. However, new keywords have been created by extensions to C, the language C++, and by the draft ANSI C standard. (C++ is a new language based on C that has greatly influenced the draft ANSI C standard. Future versions of the C standard may borrow even more from C++.) Because not all of these new keywords are known to all compilers, a program that compiles without error does not ensure that future keywords are not being misused.

The following list contains identifiers considered reserved because they are used in ANSI C, because they are traditional VAX C or pcc [1] extensions, or because they are used in C++.

---

[1] Portable C Compiler shipped with UNIX systems

_align	fortran	noalias	this
asm	friend	noshare	variant_struct
class	globaldef	operator	variant_union
const	globalref	overload	virtual
delete	globalvalue	public	void
entry	inline	readonly	volatile
enum	new	signed	

All external identifiers are reserved that match the external names used in the C library. The reason for this is that the C library is allowed to call itself to do its work. The interdependence of the external names in the library can be important; for example, *printf* may call *calloc*. Thus, a program that defines an external name duplicating one in the library may cause the entire library to stop working. The draft ANSI C standard labels such programs "undefined"; VAX C labels them "unsupported."

The draft ANSI C standard also reserves all external identifiers that begin with any of the following prefixes, where *(n)* represents a letter:

- Underscore (_)
- is*(n)*
- to*(n)*
- str*(n)*
- mem*(n)*
- wcs*(n)*

The external names in *math.h* with "f" or "l" suffixes are also reserved. Because C allows external names to be converted to one case, all lowercase, uppercase, and mixed case spellings of reserved external names are also reserved external names.

Although the draft ANSI C standard allows a reserved external identifier to be used internally by a file, it is a potentially confusing to do so. The draft ANSI C standard also reserves all identifiers that begin with an underscore followed by an uppercase letter or another underscore. Identifiers of this form are reserved not only from external use but from use internal to a file.

A.7 Definitions

In general, constants should never be coded directly; assign a meaningful name to them and assign their permanent value using a #*define* directive. This makes it much easier to administer large and evolving programs because you can change the constant value uniformly by changing the #*define* directive and recompiling.

Specify all numeric constants by #*define* directives. Exceptions to this rule are the values 0, 1, and −1 when used as relative array indices (if *p* is a pointer to an array element, *p[1]* is the next element, and *p[−1]* is the previous element).

Use compile-time computation to combine numeric constants into other constants. Be sure to put all such expressions in parentheses because the macro substitution may be requested in the middle of another expression. For example:

```
#define ARRAY_A_SIZE 123
#define ARRAY_B_SIZE 456
#define BOTH_SIZE (ARRAY_A_SIZE + ARRAY_B_SIZE)
```

If it is necessary to change ARRAY_A_SIZE, the compiler will change BOTH_SIZE without further intervention.

Often, the enumeration data type provides an improved way to manage constant definitions because the names of enumerated constants are available to the debugger. Such enumeration constants are integer constants in VAX C without the /STANDARD=PORTABLE qualifier. (They are also constants in the draft ANSI C standard.) However, if you do use the /STANDARD=PORTABLE qualifier, VAX C will warn about all operations on enumerated types beyond assignment and comparison.

The following list contains names whose meanings are standardized in C programs.

TRUE   Boolean true

FALSE   Boolean false

NULL   For comparison or assignment of pointers (defined in *stdio.h*)

EOF   End-of-file (defined in *stdio.h*)

You should use the following definitions freely and consistently:

```
#define TRUE    1
#define FALSE   0
```

The names TRUE and FALSE are used to return Boolean values from functions. Such return values may be used in Boolean expressions to control program flow. For example:

```
if (queue_not_empty(queue_header)) ...
```

On some systems, *stdio.h* contains definitions for TRUE and FALSE. In that case, do not redefine them.

Even though C logical comparisons (for example, ==, !=, >=) generate the values 0 and 1, do not use these values numerically or in a non-Boolean expression. You may assign the result of a relational to a flag (for example, *flag = pointer != NULL;*).

The proper way to test for the end of a string is by comparing the current character to a zero character constant ('\0'). Do not compare a character to the integer constant, 0, or the pointer constant, NULL. Conceptually, they are the wrong type.

NULL is defined by *stdio.h* and should not be explicitly redefined in a program.

A common problem in porting programs between operating systems is dereferencing a null (zero) pointer. On some systems, a value of 0 is stored at location 0 so programs do run and may give the correct answers. However, when these programs are ported to VMS, they fail. Therefore, programs should always test a pointer value against NULL if its value might be suspect.

A.8 Declarations

Always state types explicitly. Never leave function return values or parameters to be defaulted implicitly (that is, *int*).

Use the *const* type modifier to signal data that should not change during execution. The compiler will flag changes to such data. This data will be allocated in nonwritable, potentially shareable sections of memory.

Declare all local data using the *static* or *auto* storage classes; *auto* is implicit for variables declared within the scope of a function. However, variables declared outside the scope of a function are implicitly declared *extern*.

Explicitly declare functions that are for internal use of a specific module with the *static* storage class. (Function definitions that lack an explicit storage class are implicitly declared *extern*.)

The use of *static* or *extern* data declarations may make code non-reentrant. This is especially important for code that may need to run at AST level under VMS or as a signal handler under ULTRIX. Avoid using the *static* or *extern* storage classes if their use will produce non-reentrant code.

Whenever a type is declared that includes *function* in its type description, declare types of the function arguments. (To do this, you must use the draft ANSI C function prototype syntax. This syntax is supported by most compilers.) This rule applies not only when declaring functions, but also to pointers to functions, arrays of pointers to functions, and so on.

If a declaration is complex, use *typedef* declarations to build it out of separate parts. The next example shows the type of cryptically constructed declaration to avoid.

```
int (*(apfi[15]))(float); /* Array of pointers to functions returning
ints */
```

The next example shows how to build the definition piece by piece, which creates a much clearer declaration:

```
typedef int INT_FUNC(float);        /* Function returning int */
typedef INT_FUNC *PTR_TO_INTFUNC;   /* Pointer to int func */

PTR_TO_INTFUNC apf[15];             /* Array of function ptrs */
```

Avoid using a comma-separated list in a single declaration to declare more than one variable of the same type. A comma-separated list makes it hard to read all the variables, as shown in the following example:

```
int index, counter, sub_total, total;
```

Instead, break the list across multiple lines and align it appropriately. For example:

```
int index,
    counter,
    sub_total,
    total;
```

A.8.1 Structure Declarations

Structures enhance the logical organization of code, offer consistent addressing, and can significantly increase the efficiency and performance of C programs.

In general, if the same index addresses two or more data in a program, the data should be defined by a common structure. This design allows the program to evolve easily in the future. For instance, it becomes relatively easy to add another field to the structure or change the allocation mechanism from static to dynamic. This lets the program evolve (by adding another datum to the structure) or modify storage allocation (from compiled to dynamic).

If a program processes symbols that each have attributes such as name, type, flags, and associated value, do not define separate vectors. For example:

```
char *name[NSYMB];
int  type[NSYMB];
int  flags[NSYMB];
int  value[NSYMB];
```

Instead, define an array of structures:

```
typedef struct {
        char *name;
        int  type;
        int  flags;
        int  value;
} SYMBOL;

SYMBOL symbol_table[NSYMB];
```

In general, use *typedef* to declare *struct*s and *union*s as types. Avoid declaring a tag for a *struct* or *union* unless the *struct* or *union* is self referential, or if two or more *struct*s or *union*s are all mutually referential.

```
typedef struct LISP_LIST_TAG {
        struct LISP_LIST_TAG *car;
        struct LISP_LIST_TAG *cdr;
} LISP_LIST;
```

All other references to this structure use the *typedef* name:

```
LISP_LIST *first;               /* Pointer to a Lisp list */
```

A common C coding practice is to use the same name for the *typedef* and the *struct* or *union* tag. Because this practice conflicts with the C++ language, the coding standard described here does not allow it. In those rare cases when you need to define a tag, choose a different name from the *typedef* name of the *struct* or *union*.

A.8.2 Function Declarations

All function definitions should have a corresponding function prototype declaration. All calls to functions are to be made in the presence of a function prototype for the function being called. Most errors in argument passing can be detected by the compiler if it has the additional information provided by this type of declaration.

The proper way to obtain a function prototype for an external function that is being called is to include the appropriate header file. Function prototypes for all *static* functions in a file should be declared as part of the standard format for *.c* files described in Section A.3.

Follow the modularity rules given in Section A.2.

A.8.3 Type Compatibility

Make sure that data types are compatible throughout a program. Most cases in which data types conflict are actually programming errors. Often, you can use the type-checking capability of the VAX C compiler and the VAX Source Code Analyzer to find data type conflicts and the corresponding program logic errors.

To make it easier to maintain type compatibility, use *typedef* to declare all nonbase data types, explicit type casting where type conversion is required, and the *union* data type to combine incompatible data types.

A.8.4 Pointers

Pointers should be declared and used as "pointer to an object of type X." For example, do not use a variable that is declared as "pointer to *int*" as a pointer to a *char*.

If a pointer can point at one of a finite set of object types, it may be declared using a *union* declaration. Otherwise, use an explicit type cast to convert a pointer of one type to a pointer of another compatible type.

Integers and pointers are not compatible data types. Unfortunately, for historical reasons most C compilers will provide an implicit type cast between these two data types. However, do not consider them to be compatible types.

The draft ANSI C standard introduces a new pointer type, the generic pointer (*void *). Any pointer may be converted to and from a *void *without losing any data. This is particularly useful in assignments, function prototypes, comparisons, and conditional expressions. A *void * pointer may not be dereferenced unless it is cast to another pointer type.

VAX C implements *void * pointers. For pre-ANSI compilers that do not implement such pointers, use *char * instead.

A.9 Functions

This section describes important characteristics of functions, including definition, parameters, return values, and exception handling.

A.9.1 Definition

In general, a function is a routine that processes one or more inputs and generates one or more outputs, where each of the inputs and outputs can be described concisely. Keep functions reasonably short. This makes it easy for a maintenance engineer to read and understand all of the function at one glance. Indications that a function might be too long include a length greater than 100 lines (two pages), heavy use of localized variables (whose active scope is less than the entire function), or conditional or loop statements nested more than four levels.

Even when processing is linear (do first part, do second part), it helps the maintainability of the code if the function is broken into separate pieces. For example:

```
main(int argc, char *argv[])
{
    setup(argc, argv);
    process();
    finish();
}
```

Parameters

A function should be designed with a "natural," easy-to-remember calling sequence. Avoid functions with more than five arguments or a variable number. Avoid functions with op-code arguments, where one argument determines the number, type, and function of the others.

Describe each formal parameter in the function header comment. Use the description to indicate the type and use of the parameter, including whether the parameter (if a pointer) is used to read or modify memory.

In C, the arguments to functions are passed by value. For efficiency, avoid passing structures as parameters to functions. (On a stack machine, this will require that the contents of the structure be pushed onto the stack when you invoke the function.) Instead, functions should be declared as taking pointers to structures as parameters.

Define functions using the function prototype syntax. This approach allows you to turn the definition into a declaration by extracting the definitions with a text editor and appending a semicolon to the end.

For example:

```
static char *alloc_free_memory(int char_count);
static char *copy_string(char *source, char *target);
static char *save_string(char *string);
static int  string_length(char *eos_terminated_string);

static char *save_string(char *string)
/*
 *++
 * Description:
 *     Make a copy of a string
 *
 * Keywords:
 *     string, copy, memory allocation
 *
 * Parameters:
 *     char *string  -- (In) Pointer to the string to copy
 *
 * Side effects:
 *     Enough memory for the copy is allocated from free memory
 *
 * Exceptions:
 *     None
 *
 * Result:
 *     Character pointer to the copy of the string or NULL
 *--
 */
{
    char *cp;

    cp = alloc_free_memory(string_length(string) + sizeof(char));

    if (cp != NULL)
        copy_string(string, cp);

    return cp;
}
```

Return Values

All functions should either return a value or be explicitly declared as
a *void* function. A *void* function corresponds to a procedure in other
languages. *Void* functions are defined by the draft ANSI C standard
and may not be available in compilers that do not conform to ANSI C;
void functions are available in VAX C.

If a function computes a single value, it might be passed back to the
caller as the return value. However, it is often better to return a
status code that indicates the success or failure of the function. In
that case, any other values may be returned to the caller through

pointers provided as function arguments. Avoid functions that return structures.

Only in rare cases should a routine change the state of data other than that passed into the function as arguments or directly referenced through arguments. Any potential side effects on data not passed by an argument are to be well documented in the function header.

Because subprocesses may call programs on UNIX and VMS, all programs should exit by calling *exit( )*. On UNIX, use *exit(0)* for success and *exit(1)* for failure. On VMS, the appropriate status code should be passed to *exit( )*.

A.9.2 Exception Handling

Simple functions that do not call other functions and have well-defined exception conditions can best indicate exceptions to a caller by returning a status code as the return value of the function. For static functions, you might return a value of TRUE or FALSE, which may be used in a simple Boolean test. For external functions, return a more explicit status code.

A function can be complex, calling many other functions and potentially generating many different types of exceptions. If these routines simply returned a status code, the caller would need to perform complex analysis of the returned status code after each invocation of the function. The C language does not provide any facilities to help engineers deal with complex exception handling. However, if the program is specific to VMS, it can use the VMS condition handling facility, which does provide help.

A.10 Statements

Each line should contain only one statement. The only exception is the *else if* construct (see Section A.10.2). Note that an *if* statement and its associated conditionally executed statement appear on separate lines.

If a statement is too long for a single line, break it across lines at meaningful boundaries. Do not break symbol names across lines. You may break expressions across lines at operator boundaries, beginning the new line with the operator indented so that it aligns with the operator on the previous line. You also may break function calls at argument boundaries, beginning each line with a new argument name indented so that it lines up with the argument on the previous line.

For example:

```
rabp->rab_w_rsz = strlen(bufp->prefix)
                + strlen(bufp->text)
                + strlen(bufp->suffix)
                + sizeof(char);

status = sort_file(file_descriptor, get_next_record, put_sorted_records,
                   SORT_ASCENDING, key_descriptors);
```

Always leave a blank space between reserved words and subsequent open parenthesis, for example, *if (condition)* rather than *if(condition)*.

A.10.1 Indentation of Compound Statements

A compound statement groups declarations and statements into a single statement that is syntactically equivalent. Delimit compound statements with braces.

Set off compound statements from surrounding code to emphasize their role as single statement equivalents. Do so by using various combinations of line breaks and indentation according to personal preference. Today, C programmers commonly use two or three styles. Any one of these styles is acceptable as long as it is used consistently within a program module and when modifying the code in an existing module.

The forthcoming ANSI C standard promotes a consistent style for indenting compound statements as developed in Kernighan and Ritchie's (K&R) original book on C programming (see Appendix D). This is an acceptable indentation style. For example:

```
if (size != 0) {
    length += size;
    printf("Total length: %d", length);
}
```

Many other style guides recommend an indentation of compound statements that is common with languages that use BEGIN–END to delimit blocks. There are two main variations of this style. The first has the compound statement delimiters at outer block level; the second has them at the inner block level.

For example:

```
if (size != 0)
{
    length += size;
    printf("Total length: %d", length);
}

if (size != 0)
    {
    length += size;
    printf("Total length: %d", length);
    }
```

Individual projects should choose one of these three styles and use it consistently. The remainder of this appendix shows examples of how to format code in the K&R style and the first variation of the BEGIN-END block style, which you can easily reformat into the second variation of the BEGIN-END style.

If a compound statement is large (more than about 20 lines) or contains nested compound statements, the closing braces should be commented to indicate which block they delimit. For example:

```
for (sy = sytable; sy != NULL; sy = sy->sy_link)
{
    if (sy->sy_flag == DEFINED)
    {

        . . .

    }                   /* if defined */
    else
    {

        . . .

    }                   /* if undefined */
}                       /* for all symbols */
```

A.10.2 The *if* Statement

In its simplest form, the *if* statement contains a single, conditionally executed statement. Place this statement on a separate line and indent it one tab stop. For example:

```
if (day == monday)
    count += 7;
```

If more than one statement is required to be conditionally executed, use one of the following styles:

```
if (day == monday) {
    count += 7;
    printf("Total: %d", count);
}

if (day == monday)
{
    count += 7;
    printf("Total: %d", count);
}
```

If alternative statements are conditionally executed, you may add the *else* clause to the *if* statement. If either of the conditionally executed statements is compound, both should be compound. The following examples show the two formats.

```
if (day != monday) {
    count += 31;
} else {
    count += 7
    printf("Total: %d", count);
}

if (day != monday)
{
    count += 31;
}
else
{
    count += 7
    printf("Total: %d", count);
}
```

If the conditional test in an *if* statement is so complex that it requires more than one line, break it at an && or | | operator, and line up each expression under the preceding expression. Always enclose such conditionally executed statements in braces. For example:

```
if ((this_value == that_value)
    && (number_one != number_two)
    || (symbol_z == symbol_w)
    && (symbol_q < 10))
{
    return TRUE;
}
```

However, nested conditionals or loops should always enclose conditional or loop code in braces. Note that the following example is difficult to read:

```
for (dp = &values[0]; dp < top_value; dp++)
    if (dp->d_value == arg_value
        && (dp->d_flag & arg_flag) != 0)
        return dp;
return NULL;
```

After reformatting with braces, the example is much easier to read:

```
for (dp = &values[0]; dp < top_value; dp++)
{
    if (dp->d_value == arg_value
        && (dp->d_flag & arg_flag) != 0)
    {
        return dp;
    }
}
return NULL;
```

Although there is no separate *else if* clause in the *if* statement, it may be treated as such with the *(else if (condition))* on a single line. For example:

```
if (x == y)
    size = 0.0;
else if (x == z)
    size = 1.0;
else
    size = transform(x, y, z);
```

A.10.3   The *for* Statement

Some experience is needed to decide what to put in a *for* statement and what to put in the loop body. In general, put what is needed to control the loop in the *for* statement and the process itself in the body.

If the loop initialization is complex, place part of the initialization before the loop. Avoid separating initialization expressions with commas. If the loop control expression is complex, the use of a *while* statement may be appropriate.

If the iteration expression is complex, move part of it into the body of the *for* statement. Avoid separating iteration expressions with commas.

Another method of avoiding complexity in *for* statements is to use *break* or *continue* statements or both in the *for* statement body. However, exercise care when using these statements to control unusual break-out cases. For example, the code in the following example searches a symbol table for an unused element:

```
for (sp = &sym[0]; sp < &sym[MAX_SYM]; sp++)
{
    if ((sp->sy_flag & UNUSED) != 0)
        break;
}

if (sp >= &sym[MAX_SYM])
{
    log_error_message("The symbol table is full.");
    return FALSE;
}

/* ... here to process symbol */

...

return TRUE;
```

If the three controlling expressions of a *for* statement are long, it may help to put each of the expressions on a separate line. For example:

```
for (pointer = list_head;
     pointer != NULL && pointer->priority >= CRITICAL_PRIORITY;
     pointer = pointer->next)
```

Although the *for (;;)* statement may be used to create an indefinite loop (presumably containing a *break* or *return* statement), the preferred method is shown in the following example:

```
while (TRUE) {
    ...
}
```

Occasionally, a *for* statement or *while* statement will have a null body. To indicate this, place a semicolon on a line by itself following the *for* or *while* expression. For example:

```
for (i = 0; i < n && a[i] != key; ++i)
    ;
```

A.10.4 The *while* and *do* Statements

The simplest *while* statement contains a single loop statement. Place it on a separate line and indent it one tab stop. For example:

```
while (sp != NULL)
    sp = sp->next;
```

If more than one statement is required in the loop, use one of the following forms:

```
while (sp != NULL) {
    total_size = total_size + sp->size;
    total_length = total_length + sp->length;
}

while (sp != NULL)
{
    total_size = total_size + sp->size;
    total_length = total_length + sp->length;
}
```

If the conditional part of the *while* statement is so complex that it requires more than one line, break it at an && or || operator, and line up each expression under the preceding expression. Always enclose such conditionally executed statements in braces. For example:

```
while ((sp->next->title != NULL)
       && (sp->title_length == 0)
       && (sp->title_font != HELVETICA_HEAVY_12PT))
{
    sp = sp->next;
}
```

To clearly distinguish the *while* clause of the *do* statement from a *while* statement, always enclose the body of the *do* statement in braces. Use one of the following styles:

```
do {
    size = get_size(x, y, z);
    x = next_point(x, y, z);
} while (x == y);

do
{
    size = get_size(x, y, z);
    x = next_point(x, y, z);
} while (x == y);
```

A.10.5 The *switch* Statement

The body of the *switch* statement is enclosed in braces and indented one additional tab stop. Place each individual case clause on a new line. Indent the associated statements one additional tab stop.

All *switch* statements should have a *default* case which, if not an expected case, should signal a fatal error. The *default* case always should be last.

Try not to use the characteristic of the *switch* statement that allows a block of code associated with one case label to fall through to the block of code associated with the next case label. In those cases where it is unavoidable, make sure that it is well commented. However, you may associate several case labels that have no intervening code with one block of code. In the following example, the central algorithm of a routine counts words. A new line, blank, or tab terminates a word, but multiple blanks do not increase the number of words.

```
eow = 0;

while ((c = getchar()) != EOF)
{
    switch (c)
    {
        case '\n':                  /* Newline, */
            lines++;                /* count lines */
            /*
             * Fall through to "end of word" case
             */
        case '\t':                  /* Tabs, newlines, and blanks */
        case ' ':                   /* Form words. */
            words += eow;
            eow = 0;                /* Don't count multiple runs */
            letters++;              /* But count all "whitespace" */
            break;
        default:                    /* All the rest form a word */
            letters++;
            eow = 1;
            break;
    }
}

words += eow;                   /* Fix count of last word */
```

Note that the *break* following the last case is redundant. Nevertheless, include it to make your intention clear. Including it also reduces the likelihood that someone who adds a new case will forget to add the *break*.

The next example shows an alternative format for the preceding *switch* statement:

```
switch (c) {
    case '\n':                  /* Newline, */
        lines++;                /* count lines */
        /*
         * Fall through to "end of word" case
         */
    case '\t':                  /* Tabs, newlines, and blanks */
    case ' ':                   /* Form words. */
        words += eow;
        eow = 0;                /* Don't count multiple runs */
        letters++;              /* But count all "whitespace" */
        break;
    default:                    /* All the rest form a word */
        letters++;
        eow = 1;
        break;
}
```

A.10.6 The *goto* Statement

The use of the *goto* statement is discouraged. It is potentially confusing and programs can be written without resorting to its use.

A.11 Expressions and Operators

Because C has some operator precedence rules that differ from those of other languages, enclose all expressions that contain mixed operators in parentheses. This is particularly necessary when comparison or mask operators (&, | , and ^) are combined with shifts.

Traditionally, a C compiler can modify the order in which the operands of an expression are evaluated. In the following example, there is no guarantee that *d(&x)* is evaluated after *b(&x)* and *c(&x)* are evaluated. The C compiler could generate code that first evaluates *d(&x)*, then *b(&x)* plus *c(&x)*, and then the resulting sum.

```
a = (b(&x) + c(&x)) + d(&x);
```

The forthcoming ANSI C standard provides syntax that allows you to control evaluation order; however, the provisions are not yet final. Until C compilers follow the ANSI standard, you must write separate statements with temporary variables to ensure the evaluation order.

For example:

```
temp = b(&x) + c(&x);
a = temp + d(&x);
```

Blanks should surround all assignment operators (for example, =, +=). Using blanks helps to avoid ambiguity with some old, but still supported, operators (for example, i=-1 may be interpreted as i = -1 or i -= 1).

Blanks should appear after commas in argument lists to help separate the arguments visually. On the other hand, macros with arguments and function calls should not have a blank between the name and the left parenthesis.

C is an expression language, which means that the assignment expression $a = b$ itself has a value that can be embedded in a larger context. Use this assignment expression sparingly. The following example shows a standard C idiom.

```
while ((value = *pointer++) != 0)
{
    process(value);
}
```

Do not put a top-level assignment expression as the test expression of an *if*, *for*, or *while* statement because another engineer can easily misinterpret the assignment as a test for equality. Instead, rewrite these test expressions so that the assignment is tested explicitly against zero. The previous example illustrates this form.

Use side effects within expressions sparingly. Be suspicious of any expression in which the target of an operator with a side effect (for example, =, ++, --) appears more than once. For example, predicting the results of the code in the next example is not easy; it will do different things with different compilers.

```
func(*ptr++, *ptr++);
*ptr = *ptr++;
*ptr++ = *ptr;
```

The C language seldom guarantees the order of side effects. A compiler can evaluate the operands of most operators in any order (to allow for better optimization). For example, a compiler may evaluate the *lvalue* expression on the left-hand side of an assignment before or after it evaluates the right-hand side of the assignment. The only operators that consistently evaluate their operands left to right are the logical AND operator (&&), the logical OR operator (| |), the conditional operator (*?:*), and the comma operator (,). Note that the comma operator is not the same as the comma used to separate arguments to a function. A function call may have its arguments evaluated in any order. Also note that the logical and conditional operators are guaranteed to evaluate only those operands needed to determine the value of the expression.

Whenever conditional sequences contain both | | and &&, use parentheses to make the sequences clearer.

Use the increment (++) and decrement (--) operators sparingly. You may use them when they are the only operators in a statement or when the only additional operator is the simple assignment operator. You may also use them in the iteration expression of the *for* statement. For example:

```
--count;

i = count++;

for (i = 0; i < 10; i++)
    count += array[i];
```

A.12 Portability

C is often the language of choice for many new software applications because it is widely available and supported by a number of operating systems. However, you need to be aware of some of the potential problems that arise when porting C programs and should consider the following issues:

- Most C compilers predefine symbols that may be used to isolate machine-dependent code. For example, VAX C predefines the following symbols: *VAX, vax, VMS, vms, ultrix.*

NOTE

The draft ANSI C standard may require that VAX C change the names of these predefined symbols in the future. The VAX C compiler also supports the /DEFINE qualifier under VMS and the –Dxxx option under ULTRIX to predefine a symbol without modifying the source code.

- Different machines have different word sizes. Although the language guarantees that *long int* is at least as long as *int*, and *short int* is never longer than *int*, it does not guarantee any specific word length. Note that pointers and integers are not necessarily the same size nor are all pointers the same size.

  If you transport programs in which *int* and *long* sizes differ, double-check *printf* format statements. Some *printf* implementations require %ld for longs, while others require %D.

- Word size and constants can interact in unexpected ways. The following example clears the low order three bits of an integer on a PDP–11. However, on a VAX, it also clears the upper halfword.

```
int x;
x &= 0177770;
```

Instead use the following code, which is portable:

```
x &= ~07;
```

- Use parentheses to ensure the order of evaluation. Avoid the following sequences:

```
value = getchar() - getchar();

value = *p++ - *p++;

*p = *p++;

func(*p++, *p++);
```

In these sequences, different compilers evaluate the expressions in different orders. Instead, rewrite these as shown in the next example:

```
value = getchar();
value -= getchar();

value = *p++;
value -= *p++;

p[1] = *p;
p++;

temp = *p++;
func(temp, *p++);
```

- Do not use code that takes advantage of two's complement arithmetic. In particular, avoid optimizations that replace division or multiplication with shifts.
- Be aware that the VAX signed character may become unsigned on many other machines. If it matters whether characters are signed or not, explicitly use the types *signed char* or *unsigned char* instead of *char*.
- Do not assume any specific byte or bit ordering within words.

- Be aware that some constructs that normally return a Boolean result in other languages do not return a Boolean in C. An example of incorrect code follows:

```
if (strcmp(s1, s2))
{
    /* different */
}
```

Strcmp does not return TRUE or FALSE; instead, it returns a negative value to indicate s1 is less than s2, zero to indicate that the strings are equal, or a positive value to indicate that s1 is greater than s2. Therefore, the result of *strcmp* should always be compared against zero. For example:

```
if ((strcmp(s1, s2) >= 0)
{
    /* s1 greater than or equal to s2 */
}
```

- The bitwise logical operators in C have the wrong precedence to test for a value of a specific bit without using parentheses. For example:

```
if (flag_word & MASK == INTERESTING_BIT)
```

The preceding section of code would be interpreted as follows:

```
if (flag_word & (MASK == INTERESTING_BIT))
```

You must use parentheses to be sure that the code is evaluated correctly. For example:

```
if ((flag_word & MASK) == INTERESTING_BIT)
```

- Be suspicious of numeric values appearing in the code. Almost all constants are better expressed as *#define* quantities.
- Become familiar with the standard library and use it for string and character manipulation. Do not reimplement standard routines because the person reading the code must then determine whether the reimplemented code does something special. Locally developed "standard" routines are a frequent source of errors because these routines may be called by other parts of the library. Furthermore, the standard library hides nonportable details that you might not be aware of.

International Product Development

To be competitive in today's marketplace, it is becoming increasingly important to design products for international distribution. This appendix presents a model and summarizes guidelines for international product development.

B.1   International Product Model

The international product model used at Digital describes a software system that functions interactively. The model also assumes that customers use the system in a local environment, that is, using local languages (French, German, and others), conventions, and user interfaces. Such software is said to be localized.

The purpose of the model, shown in Figure B–1 is to identify the components of international products.

In building international products, some portions or components remain constant, while others change. The constant portion is called the international base component, which represents the components that are applicable worldwide. The portions that vary between countries or markets are the user interface components, market-specific components, and the country-specific components.

Figure B–1:   International Product Model

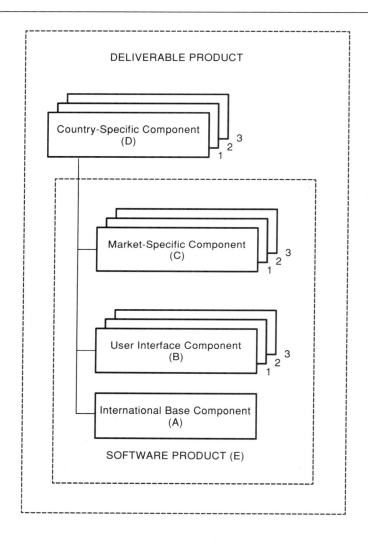

The engineering, packaging, and distribution of these components may vary due to specific product or market requirements. However, it is important to keep the integrity of the components intact to produce a more flexible product that is easy for local engineering groups to adapt.

Separating the product into components makes it easier to develop country, market, and user-language variations. It also reduces both the development costs and maintenance costs of the product variations. This component structuring scheme also adds significant flexibility in the software packages offered worldwide.

During a product's development, the cross-functional team should verify requirements for the content of each of the components. The members of the cross-functional team must agree upon responsibilities for the different components. The functional capabilities of these components must be well defined. For example, the original engineering group may agree to produce one country-specific component, and local engineering groups may agree to develop other translated country-specific components. The product requirements, specification, and development plan should clearly state what product characteristics will be developed and supported and by whom.

The next sections define the terms used in the model.

International Base Component
This component consists of common modules whose generalized code is applicable worldwide (with user-selected variants) without change. Alternatively, this component may have external controls that provide the variations required in an international product. Typically, the international base component has no information about the language employed to communicate with the user.

User Interface Component
This component contains information about the language employed to communicate with the user. It is a language-specific component that functions as a translation layer for processing input and output text in the language of the user. For example, this component could process user information, such as user messages, online help, and documentation.

Market-Specific Component

This component provides features that make the product competitive in a particular market or area. A market can be driven by regional or country requirements as well as needs for specific features. For example, the general market requirements for an office system would be satisfied in the international base component; the market-specific component could contain the modem, printer, local interconnect, and power cords, which tend to vary by region or country. Because the market-specific component must interface with the international base component, both require a modular design with precisely defined interfaces, including functional and performance specifications.

Country-Specific Component

This component contains information that is specific to a certain country and is required before the product can be delivered locally. It does not contain any code. Typical contents are warranties, service and ordering information, license certificates, and terms and conditions.

Product Variations

Product variations refer to a range of products that have a common base component but have different user interfaces and market-specific components. Product variations do not have a country-specific component.

Software Product

The software product is one of a set of product variations. It combines components that can be ordered and manufactured.

Deliverable Product

The deliverable product combines a product variation with a country-specific component to provide a product that is ready for delivery to the customer.

B.2 International Software Design Guidelines

Use the following guidelines when developing software for international markets:

- To allow easier translation, separate input and output text in the user interface from the code that presents it.

- Use table-driven and modular replacement techniques to design code for the international base and market-specific components that can be easily adapted to international requirements.

- During design, separate the code for the user interface in distinct modules. This will allow the user interface code to be modified easily for specific user languages without affecting the bulk of the product's functions. Use a forms management system such as DECforms as the base for the user interface controller.

- Design for consistent functional and user interface behavior across the various operating systems on which distributed software solutions will be produced.

- Follow the international product model shown in Figure B–1.

Appendix C

Industry Standards

This appendix summarizes IEEE standards of interest to software engineers. It also lists suppliers of other standards.

C.1 IEEE Standards

For more information on any of the IEEE standards listed below, see the *Software Engineering Standards*, published in 1987 by The Institute of Electrical and Electronics Engineers, Inc., 345 East 47th Street, New York, New York 10017, USA.

Std 729-1983: Glossary of Software Engineering Terminology

This standard defines more than 500 software engineering terms commonly used in the field. Its use helps provide consistency in terminology.

Std 730-1984: Software Quality Assurance Plans

This standard attempts to meet concerns for legal liability. It addresses the needs of software applications whose failure could result in significant financial or social loss. The standard describes planned steps on a project that would allow a development team to be assured that the application meets established technical requirements. Further, it provides a format and minimum contents for Software Quality Assurance Plans.

Std 828-1983: Software Configuration Management Plans

This standard provides engineers with those requirements that are necessary for configuration identification and control, status accounting and reporting, and configuration audits and reviews.

Std 829-1983: Software Test Documentation

The complete testing process is encompassed by eight documents whose format and content are described by this standard. Three areas are discussed: the test plan, the test specification, and test reporting. The standard describes the extent, resources, and schedule of the testing activities. Further, it describes items to be tested, functionality to be tested, tasks to be completed, people who carry out the tasks, and the plan risks.

Std 830-1984: Software Requirements Specifications

This standard provides different ways to specify software requirements. Tutorial material describes specification methods and formats.

Std 983-1986: Software Quality Assurance Planning

This standard explains the sections of the Software Quality Assurance Plan as described in Std 730-1984.

Std 990-1986: Ada as a Program Design Language

This standard recommends ways to effectively use program design languages using Ada as the programming language.

Std 1002-1987: Taxonomy for Software Engineering Standards

This standard explains how to classify software engineering standards based on their form and content.

Std 1008-1987: Software Unit Testing

This standard provides an integrated approach to system testing.

Std 1012-1986: Software Verification and Validation Plans

This standard describes minimum requirements for the content and form of Software Verification and Validation Plans (SVVPs).

Std 1016-1987: Software Design Descriptions

This standard describes what to put in and how to organize software design documents.

C.2 Sources for Other Standards

This section contains supplier information for the following categories of standards:

- Industry: Standards and technical papers from associations and organizations such as IEEE
- Military: Documents in the public domain, including military specifications, standards, and handbooks
- Government: Documents from all branches of the federal government, including federal specifications and standards. This includes the following two series of documents published by the National Bureau of Standards (NBS) in the U.S. Department of Commerce:
  - Federal Information Processing Standards Publication series (FIPS PUBs)
  - Computer Science and Technology (NBS Special Publication 500-xx series)
- Foreign: Non-U.S. standards, such as British, German (DIN), International Organization for Standardization (ISO), and International Electrotechnical Commission (IEC)

Suppliers

American National Standards Institute (ANSI)
ANSI represents most foreign country specifications and supplies all types of national standards. Although industry standards are available, ANSI does not carry military and government standards.

> 1430 Broadway
> New York, NY 10018
> (212) 642–4900 (sales/ordering)
> (212) 354–3300

Document Center
This center supplies industry, military, and government specifications and standards.

> 1504 Industrial Way, Unit 9
> Belmont, CA 94002
> (415) 591–7600

Document Engineering
This group supplies military and government standards and specifications.

15210 Stagg Street
Van Nuys, CA 91405
(818) 782–1010

Global Engineering
This group supplies industry, military, government, and foreign specifications and standards.

2625 Hickory Street
Santa Ana, CA 92707
(800) 854–7179
(714) 540–9870

Information Handling Service
This group supplies industry, military, and government specifications and standards. IHS puts information on microfilm, microfiche, or on line.

15 Inverness Way East
Inglewood, CO 80150
(800) 525–7052
(303) 790–0600

National Standards Association
This association supplies industry, military, and government specifications and standards.

5161 River Road
Bethesda, MD 20816
(800) 638–8094
(301) 951–1389

Naval Publications and Forms Center

The center supplies limited quantities of military, government, and some industry specifications, standards, and handbooks. Documents are free of charge.

5801 Tabor Avenue
Philadelphia, PA 19120-5009
(215) 697–3321 (shipment by first-class mail)
(215) 697–4834 (shipment by Federal Express)

U.S. Government Printing Office

This agency supplies U.S. government publications, including specifications and standards.

Superintendent of Documents
U.S. Government Printing Office
Washington D.C. 20402

Appendix **D**

Additional Reading

This appendix lists titles and tells how to order the documents and books referenced throughout this guide. These resources are divided into two main sections:

- Applications and tools
- Software development

The listings are alphabetical within each section. There is a table at the end of this appendix showing you how to order documentation from Digital.

D.1   Applications and Tools

Guide to VAX DEC/Code Management System
Order No. AI–KL03A–TE

Guide to VAX DEC/Module Management System
Order No. AI–P119C–TE

Guide to VAX DEC/Test Manager
Order No. AI–Z330C–TE

Guide to VAX Language-Sensitive Editor and VAX Source Code Analyzer
Order No. AI–FY24B–TE

Guide to VAX Notes
Order No. AI–G98HA–TE

Guide to VAX Performance and Coverage Analyzer
Order No. AI–EB54D–TE

Guide to VAX SCAN
Order No. AI–FU79B–TE

Guide to VAX Software Project Manager
Order No. AI–KP49A–TE

Guide to VMS Programming Resources
Order No. AA–LA57A–TE

Introduction to VMS System Routines
Order No. AA–LA66A–TE

A Methodology for Software Development Using VMS Tools
Order No. AA–HB16B–TE

This document describes how to use VMS tools with other VMS facilities to create an effective software development environment.

VAX CDD/Plus Common Dictionary Operator Reference Manual
Order No. AA–KL45A–TE

VAX CDD/Plus Common Dictionary Operator User's Guide
Order No. AA–KL46A–TE

VAX C Run-Time Library Reference Manual
Order No. AI–JP84A–TE

This manual provides reference information on the VAX C Run-Time Library (RTL) functions and macros that provide I/O functionality, character and string manipulation, mathematical functionality, error detection, subprocess creation, system access, and windowing capabilities.

VAX DOCUMENT User Manual, Volume 1
VAX DOCUMENT User Manual, Volume 2
Step-by-Step: Writing with VAX DOCUMENT
Order Nos. AA–JT84A–TE, AA–JT84A–TE, AA–JT85A–TE

VAX Text Processing Utility Manual
Order No. AA–LA14A–TE

VMS Command Definition Utlity Manual
Order No. AA–LA60A–TE

VMS Message Utility Manual
Order No. AA–LA63A–TE

VMS RTL Screen Management (SMG$) Manual
Order No. AA–LA77A–TE

VMS Run-Time Library Routines Manual
Order No. AA–76A–TE

VMS Utility Routines Manual
Order No. AA–LA67A–TE

VMS Debugger Manual
Order No. AA–LA59A–TE

VAX GKS/OB V3.0 Document Set
Order No. QA–810AA–GZ; includes the following:

> *VAX GKS Reference Manual Volume 1*
> *VAX GKS Reference Manual Volume 2*
> *VAX GKS User Manual*
> *Writing VAX GKS Handlers*
> *VAX GKS Pocket Guide*

VAX PHIGS V1.1 Document Set
Order No. QA–0KBAA–GZ; includes the following:

> *VAX PHIGS PHIGS$ Binding Manual*
> *VAX PHIGS FORTRAN Binding Manual*
> *VAX PHIGS C Binding Manual*
> *VAX PHIGS Reference Manual*

DECforms Document Set
Order No. QA–VCHAA–GZ; includes the following:

> *DECforms Guide to Developing Forms*
> *DECforms Guide to Programming*
> *DECforms Reference Manual*
> *DECforms Guide to Converting VAX FMS Applications*
> *DECforms Guide to Converting VAX TDMS Applications*

DECforms Summary Card
DECforms Keypad Card

VMS DECwindows User Kit
Order No. QA–09SAB–GZ; includes the following:

VMS DECwindows User's Guide
VMS DECwindows Desktop Applications Guide
Overview of VMS DECwindows

VMS DECwindows Programming Kit
Order No. QA–001AM–GZ; includes the following:

XUI Style Guide
VMS DECwindows Guide to Application Programming
VMS DECwindows User Interface Language Reference Manual
VMS DECwindows Toolkit Routines Reference Manual Part 1
VMS DECwindows Toolkit Routines Reference Manual Part 2
VMS DECwindows Guide to Xlib Programming: MIT C Binding
VMS DECwindows Guide to Xlib Programming: VAX Binding
VMS DECwindows Xlib Routines Reference Manual Part 1
VMS DECwindows Xlib Routines Reference Manual Part 2
VMS DECwindows Device Driver Manual
VMS Compound Document Architecture Manual

ULTRIX–32W (DECwindows) V1.1 Document Set
Order No. QA–0JQAA–GZ; includes the following:

UWS (ULTRIX Workstation Software) V2.0 Release notes
UWS Advanced Installation Guide
UWS Guide to UWS Window Manager
UWS Reference Pages, Section 1
UWS Introduction to UWS User Environment
UWS DECwindows User's Guide
UWS DECwindows Desktop Applications Guide
UWS Guide to DXDIFF VS DIFF Programming
UWS XUI Programming Overview
UWS Guide to Writing Applications for Widgets
UWS Guide to Porting Xlib Applications
UWS Guide to DXDB Debugger
UWS Guide to XUI User Interface
UWS Guide to XUI Toolkit Widgets
UWS Guide to Toolkit Intrinsics

UWS Guide to Xlib Library
UWS X Window System Protocol
UWS Reference Pages Section 3
UWS Guide to X Toolkit Widgets
UWS User Interface Style Guide

D.2 Software Development

The Art of Software Testing
Myers, Glenford J. New York, N.Y.: John Wiley and Sons, 1979.

Discusses the purpose and nature of software testing. Contains information on test tools, debugging, code inspections, as well as techniques for high level testing.

CASE: Using Software Development Tools
Fisher, Alan S. New York, N.Y.: John Wiley and Sons, 1988.

A recent overview of computer-aided software engineering technologies and commercially available third-party CASE tools. Includes tools that support analysis and design phases.

The Digital Dictionary
Marotta, Robert E., ed. Bedford, Mass.: Digital Press, 1986.
Order No. EY–3433E–DP

This document provides definitions for the terminology and acronyms specific to Digital's products and working guidelines.

Guide to Creating VMS Modular Procedures
Order No. AA–FB84A–TE

This useful guide is part of the VMS documentation set. It describes how to design and code procedures that conform to the VMS Modular Programming Standard. It also describes how to insert modules into an object module library, shareable image, or shareable image library.

Software Engineering: A Practitioner's Approach, 2nd Edition
Pressman, Roger S. New York, N.Y.: McGraw-Hill, 1987.

An excellent and widely used textbook covering the fundamentals of software design and management.

Software Engineering Standards
This book contains eleven standards relevant to the software engineering process. Its purpose is to provide guidelines and recommendations for the development and maintenance of software. Contact:

> The Institute of Electrical and Electronics Engineers, Inc.
> 345 East 47th Street
> New York, NY 10017

Structured Techniques for Computing
Martin, James, and Carma McClure. Englewood Cliffs, N.J.: Prentice-Hall, 1985.

Discusses strategies and techniques of structured analysis and design including several design methodologies such as Yourdon and Warnier, Orr.

The C Programming Language
Kernighan, Brian W., and Ritchie, Dennis M. Englewood Cliffs, N.J.: Prentice-Hall, 1978.

Contains a tutorial on the C programming language as well as detailed examples.

How to Order Documentation from Digital

From	Call	Write
Alaska, Hawaii, or New Hampshire	603–884–6660	Digital Equipment Corporation P.O. Box CS2008 Nashua, NH 03061
Rest of U.S.A. and Puerto Rico*	1–800–DIGITAL	

* Prepaid orders from Puerto Rico, Call Digital's local subsidiary (809–754–7575)

Canada	800–267–6219 (for software documentation) 613–592–5111 (for hardware documentation)	Digital Equipment of Canada Ltd. 100 Herzberg Road Kanata, Ontario, Canada K2K 2A6 Attn: Direct Order Desk

Trademarks

The following are trademarks of Digital Equipment Corporation.

DDIF	LN03 ScriptPrinter	VAX FORTRAN
DEC/CMS	MicroVAX	VAX MACRO
DEC/MMS	PrintServer	VAX Notes
DECnet	ULTRIX	VAX RALLY
DECnet–VAX	VAX C	VAX RMS
DECstation	VAX CDD	VAX SCAN
DECSYSTEM-20	VAX COBOL GENERATOR	VAXmate
DECwindows	VAX DEC/Test Manager	VAXstation
DECwrite	VAX DATATRIEVE	VMS Debugger
EDT	VAX DIBOL	VT
LN03	VAX DOCUMENT	WPS–PLUS
LN03 PLUS	VAXELN	XUI

The following are third-party trademarks.

MS–DOS is a registered trademark of Microsoft Corporation.

OS/2 is a trademark of International Business Machines Corporation.

POSTSCRIPT is a registered trademark of Adobe Systems, Inc.

UNIX is a registered trademark of American Telephone & Telegraph Company.

X Window System is a trademark of the Massachusetts Institute of Technology.

Index

229

C language (cont'd.)
    external specification as *.h* file • 176
    function definitions in • 179
    functions in • 190 to 193
    header files • 179 to 180
    .h file organization • 179
    implementation as *.c* file • 176
    modular programming • 176
    module organization • 178, 179
    naming conventions for • 181 to 184
    portability issues • 186, 204 to 206
    reserved identifiers in • 183 to 184
    reserved name in • 183
    source files • 178 to 179
        for implementation part of C module • 176
        line length conventions • 178
        organization of • 178
    tools for • 176
    use of form feed • 178
C language compiler
    error messages • 175
    predefined symbols for • 204
    STANDARD=PORTABLE qualifier • 176, 185
C language statements • 193 to 202
    do, formatting • 199 to 200
    for, formatting • 197 to 199
    goto, use of • 202
    if, formatting • 196 to 197
    indentation • 194 to 195
    switch, formatting • 200 to 201
    while, formatting • 199 to 200
Client image
    naming convention for • 117
CMS
    See DEC/CMS
Code Management System
    See DEC/CMS
code reDesign review
    for maintenance • 162
Code review • 123 to 126
    for maintenance • 163
    formal inspection • 124
    guidelines for inspection • 125
    walkthrough • 123
Coding guidelines • 93 to 126
    See also C language; Naming conventions
    choice of language • 107

Coding guidelines (cont'd.)
    formatting • 106
    for readability • 108 to 114
    for reused code • 94
    goals • 93
    scope • 93
    sources of • 93 to 95
Cohesion
    in module design • 95
Command Definition Utility • 35
Comment
    block • 112
    bracketed • 114
    case conventions for • 109
    formatting with LSE • 114, 163
    line • 112, 114
    trailing • 114
    types of • 180
Common Data Dictionary
    See VAX CDD/PLUS
Communication within project
    tools for • 161
Configuration management
    See Software configuration management
Constants, defining in C • 185
Control program
    naming convention for • 117
Conventions
    See Coding guidelines; Naming conventions
Copyright
    in module preface • 95, 96
Coverage
    by VAX Performance and Coverage Analyzer •
        132
    for tests • 130, 132
Creation date
    in module preface • 98
Customer services representative • 5

D

Data definitions in C module • 178
Data dictionary
    See VAX CDD/PLUS
Data flow diagram
    use in design document • 88

Data structure definition
    naming convention for • 122
Data types
    compatibility in C • 189, 190
DCL commands
    command files use for testing • 138
    use for counting lines of code • 172
    use for defining syntax • 35
    use with Command Definition Utility • 35
Debugger
    See VMS Debugger
DEC/CMS • 18 to 19
    change history • 98
    overview • 18
    use for build procedures • 90
    use for maintenance • 157, 165, 167, 170
DEC/MMS • 20
    features • 20
    overview • 20
    use for build procedures • 90
    use for maintenance • 157, 164
DEC/Test Manager • 16 to 17
    features • 17
    overview • 16
    test organization • 134
    use for coverage analysis • 130
    use for maintenance • 157, 169 to 170
    use for regression testing • 17, 136, 168
    use for white box tests • 132
DECforms Document Set • 222
DEC GKS
    See DEC GKS • 73
Declaration
    See Module declaration
Declarations
    C-specific • 186 to 190
    functions in C • 189
    structure of for C • 188
DEC PHIGS • 74
DECwindows • 71 to 75
    architecture • 71
    features • 71
    goals • 71
    network transparency • 74
    run-time libraries • 72
    user interface • 72
DECwrite • 33

Definitions
    use of in C • 185 to 186
Design
    See also Detailed design
        High-level design
        User interface
    and LSE use • 162
    documentation for maintenance • 161
    for performance • 139
    for testing • 133
    levels of • 64
Design and implementation
    overview • 84
Design and implementation phase • 8, 83 to 92
Design methodology • 224
    choosing • 66
    Yourdon • 66
Design review
    guidelines • 75 to 77
    process • 75
    walkthrough • 123
Detailed design
    See also Design
    compared to high-level design • 63
    inputs and outputs • 86
Detailed design document • 59
    purpose • 88
Development plan • 58
Development team
    See also Engineering project leader
    common problems with assignments • 48
    members of • 45
    overview • 45, 49
    responsibilities of • 49
Digital Command Language commands
    See DCL commands
DIGITAL Standard Runoff • 30 to 31
Digital standards
    calling and condition handling • 78
    modular programming • 80
Directory
    naming convention for • 118
Directory structure
    using logical names • 158
DOCUMENT
    See VAX DOCUMENT

231

Formatting code
    LSE language examples • 106
Form feed
    to separate C code sections • 178
    to separate C function definitions • 179
    to separate header file sections • 179
    to separate routines • 110
For statement, C formatting • 197 to 199
Functional description
    in module procedure • 102
Functional design
    levels of • 64
Functional test
    organizing with • 134
Functional value
    calling standard definition • 79
Function declarations
    in C • 189
Function definitions
    order in C module • 179
Functions in C
    definition of • 190
    exception handling • 193
    parameters of • 191
    return value • 192

G

GKS
    See DEC GKS
Global routines
    naming in C • 182
Global variable
    See Variable
goto statement, use in C • 202
Graphics editor • 33
Guidelines
    See Coding guidelines; Design review
Guide to Creating VMS Modular Procedures • 223
Guide to VAX DEC/Code Management System • 219
Guide to VAX DEC/Module Management System •
    219
Guide to VAX DEC/Test Manager • 219
*Guide to VAX Language-Sensitive Editor and VAX
    Source Code Analyzer* • 219
Guide to VAX Notes • 219

Guide to VAX Performance and Coverage Analyzer •
    220
Guide to VAX SCAN • 220
Guide to VAX Software Project Manager • 220
Guide to VMS Programming Resources • 220

H

Header files
    including in C • 179
    organization of • 179 to 180
Help file
    naming convention for • 117
.h file
    external specification of C module • 176
.h files
    See C language header files
High-level design
    description • 62 to 64
High-level design document • 59
Human interface
    design of • 67 to 75

I

IDENTIFIER string • 116
IEEE standards • 81, 213
If expression
    LSE example of use • 106
If statement, C formatting • 196 to 197
Image file ID
    naming convention • 122
Image name field
    naming convention • 123
Implementation language • 107
Implicit input
    in module procedure • 103
INCLUDE file
    in module declaration • 99
Incremental testing
    See Testing
Initialization file
    naming convention for • 117
Inspection, formal
    See also Code review; Design review
Integrated testing • 131

Modification history
    with DEC/CMS • 98
Modular Programming Standard • 80 to 81
Module
    See also Module declaration; Module preface;
        Module procedure
    definition of • 95
    design of • 95
    header for • 96, 178, 179
    LSE C template for • 104
    LSE placeholder for • 96
    naming convention for • 119
    naming in C • 183
    organization of for C • 176, 178
Module declaration
    components of • 99 to 101
    template for • 99
Module Management System
    See DEC/MMS
Module preface
    components of • 96 to 99
    template for • 96
Module procedure
    components of • 101 to 104
    template for • 101
Module statement
    in module preface • 96

N

Naming conventions
    description • 115 to 123
    directories • 118
    file image IDs • 122 to 123
    file names • 115
    file types • 116
    in C • 181 to 184
    modules • 119
    objects • 122
    procedures • 118 to 119
    use for maintenance • 159
    variables • 120 to 121
Notes conferences
    See VAX Notes
    for project communication • 161
    use for maintenance • 158

O

Object library
    naming convention for • 117
Operators
    increment and decrement use C • 204
    use of parentheses in C • 202
Option file
    naming convention for • 117
Overhead
    allowance for in schedule • 50, 51

P

Parameter
    See Formal parameters
Parameters in C • 191
Parentheses
    use in C expressions • 202, 203 to 206
PCA
    See VAX Performance and Coverage Analyzer
Performance and Coverage Analyzer
    See VAX Performance and Coverage Analyzer
Performance debugging
    during maintenance • 170
Performance problems
    locating with VAX PCA • 140
Performance testing • 139 to 142
    criteria for user interface • 69
    guidelines • 142
Phase review meeting
    purpose of • 3
Phase review process
    characteristics • 1
    illustration of • 1
    overview • 1 to 9
PHIGS
    See DEC PHIGS • 74
Physical design • 87
Placeholders
    See LSE, placeholders
Planning and preliminary design phase • 7, 61 to
    82
Pointers
    use of in C • 190

Polling for field test
  See Field test
Portability of C • 186, 204 to 206
Precedence in C expressions • 202, 205, 206
Preface
  See Module preface
Problem report maintenance • 166
Procedure
  See Module procedure
Product evaluation report
  contents • 152
Productivity
  improving • 171
  metrics of • 171
Product kits
  See Kits
Product manager • 5
Product requirements document • 56 to 57
Product specification • 57 to 58
Product team
  members • 43
  responsibilities • 4, 44
Program design language
  alternatives • 88
Progress reports • 48
Project account and conferences • 161
Project control
  model for • 53
  process for • 53
Project documentation • 54 to 60
  alternatives/feasibility study • 57
  detailed design document • 59
  development plan • 58
  field test plan • 60
  field test report • 60
  high-level design document • 59
  marketing requirements document • 56
  product requirements document • 56
  product specifications • 57
Project leader
  responsibilities of • 46
Project leader, engineering
  managing base levels • 89
Project management • 43 to 60
  See also VAX Software Project Manager
  design for • 50

Project meeting
  role in communication • 161
Project planning
  tasks for • 49
Project schedule
  preparing • 49
  strategies for • 51
  VAX Software Project Manager use for • 54
Project team
  See Development team
Prototype
  and early evaluation field test • 148
  goals and process • 66
  use • 67
PSECT
  naming convention for • 122
Pseudocode
  use in design document • 88

Q

Qualification • 145 to 153
Qualification phase • 8
Qualifying the design for production • 8
Quality and communication • 160
Queue name
  naming convention for • 122

R

Readability guidelines • 108 to 114
Registers
  calling standard definition • 79
Registration
  of file types • 116
Regression testing • 17, 135 to 139, 140
  causes of failure • 91
  during maintenance • 168
Release notes, purpose of • 152
Release notes file
  naming convention for • 117
Requirements
  and field test • 145
  for user interface design • 68
  gathering in early evaluation field test • 148
Reserved identifiers
  in C • 183 to 184

Resource materials • 219 to 225
Retirement phase • 9
Return values in C • 192
Review
    See Code review; Design review
Rights data base identifier
    naming convention for • 122
Risk assessment
    during design • 86
RTL image file
    naming convention for • 117
Runoff
    See DIGITAL Standard Runoff
Run-time library
    See VAX C RTL; VMS RTL

S

Sales impact • 7
Sales representative • 5
SCA
    See VAX Source Code Analyzer
SCAN
    See VAX SCAN
Schedule
    See Project schedule
Screen management routines • 37
Server image
    naming convention for • 117
Shareable image
    image ID naming convention for • 123
Shareable image file
    naming convention for • 117
Side effect
    in module procedure • 103
    use in C expressions • 203
Software configuration management • 18, 20
    See also DEC/CMS
Software Engineering Standards • 224
Software life cycle
    overview • 1 to 9
Source Code Analyzer
    See VAX Source Code Analyzer
Source files
    See also C language source files
    file length conventions • 178

Source files (cont'd.)
    organization of • 178 to 179
Spacing
    around C operators • 202
    use for code readability • 110, 111
Specification, product • 57 to 58
Standards • 213 to 217
    IEEE • 81, 213
    other, sources of • 215
Startup file
    naming convention for • 117
Status code
    naming convention for • 122
Storage allocation
    in module declaration • 100
Strategy and requirements phase • 4
Structure chart
    use in design document • 88
Structure declarations
    for C • 188
Switch statement, C formatting • 200 to 201
Symbols
    predefined in C • 204
    use of • 109

T

Table of contents
    in module declaration • 99
Task work
    planning by team members • 47
    problems • 48
    status report of • 48
Team meetings • 49
Template directories
    in DEC/Test Manager • 169
Testing • 127 to 143
    See also Performance testing
    coverage for • 130, 132
    DEC/Test Manager descriptions for • 138
    design for • 133
    goals of • 127
    guidelines, error • 142
    guidelines, performance • 142
    guidelines, summary of • 142
    high-level • 64
    incremental • 131

W

X